THE MEMORIAL IN THE SCHOOL

THE MEMORIAL IN THE SCHOOL

*The Story of the Teachers and Pupils from
Kirkcaldy High School who died in the Great War*

John S B Beck

Reveille
PRESS

Reveille Press is an imprint of
Tommies Guides Military Booksellers & Publishers

Gemini House
136–140 Old Shoreham Road
Brighton
BN3 7BD

www.tommiesguides.co.uk

First published in Great Britain by
Reveille Press 2014

For more information please visit
www.reveillepress.com

A catalogue record for this book is available
from the British Library

ISBN 978-1-908336-85-9

Cover design by Reveille Press
Typeset by Vivian@Bookscribe

Printed and bound in Great Britain

CONTENTS

PART III

FOREWORD

Much will be written about the so called Great War, in this, the centenary year of its onset. Most contributors will view events through one tinted lens or other, usually depending on political prejudice. What John Beck has done in this slim volume is very different. For this work is focused solely on the brief lives, and deaths, of young men, associated with a school in Kirkcaldy – a town which in 1914 was the foremost centre of industry and commerce in Fife, that peninsular kingdom on Scotland's eastern coast.

These are the brief biographies of a school community's war dead – their names beautifully cast in bronze, forming the stylish memorial which sits at the heart of Kirkcaldy High School to this day. As current Rector of the school, it is a great privilege to be asked to make this small contribution to an important work.

Kirkcaldy High School was, in 1914, the successor to the "Burgh" school. In effect, it was a grammar school, where any "lad o' pairts" could prosper and develop the skills and knowledge required to serve the global, national or local interests of the British Empire. Many did, and with great success, the school being widely regarded as one of the best of its kind in Scotland. Based on a strong democratic tradition, and rooted in the sixteenth century parish school system - Kirkcaldy High School's first iteration dates from 1582 - these schools were a treasured part of Scottish life.

Then came the Great War – its merciless toll so poignantly measured out here. For me, the very brevity, and sometimes the banality, of the vignettes assembled by John Beck accentuate the brutality of the War. Death had clearly become a workaday event. However, it is never difficult to feel for the bereft families living in streets known to us today, many nearby our current campus, often with familiar family names, many still on the school roll; sons and brothers lost, "happy, bright and winsome" laddies destroyed.

That egalitarian tradition of Scotland's education system is clearly reflected in these biographies – captains and corporals, surgeons and sergeants, they died together. Bullets, gas and shells respected no social status. And today, historians agree that the impersonal, even industrial, nature of the war laid the foundations for the strong social progress and democratisation which marked the early and middle years of the 20th Century.

As a child my granny would occasionally allow me the honour of viewing her long dead brother's medals, kept so lovingly in the brass tobacco tin presented to servicemen by Princess Mary at Christmas 1914. He was a Seaforth Highlander, and like many of the Kirkcaldy boys, he didn't survive the Somme. Neither did the telegram our family received – "died of wounds" it said. Enough said. John Beck's work is remarkable, and the simplicity of its intent is its strength. No comment is necessary. These stark, sometimes terse, accounts of lives cut short speak very loudly.

To this day our school community feels somehow marked by 1914-18. The very prominent position of our war memorial and its sheer scale ensure impact, however subtly felt. Every November we hold a ceremony of remembrance hosting serving soldiers, airmen and sailors, who lay poppy wreaths. Our young people are part of it. They respect the sacrifice of those named in bronze. We are proud of them all.

Fading away like the stars in the morning
Losing their light in the glorious sun
Thus would we pass from this earth and its toiling
Only remembered for what we have done
(Traditional)

Derek Allan
Rector of Kirkcaldy High School
March 2014

ACKNOWLEDGEMENTS

This book is the product of many people's efforts. Some are known to me but this record could not have been produced without contributions from professional and amateur researchers, archivists both paid and unpaid, and help and advice from genealogists. I therefore acknowledge the help and assistance given by the following persons:

Sheila Campbell (Local Studies and Family History Librarian) for her work with the photographs, Ruth Reed (Archives Manager, Royal Bank of Scotland Group, Edinburgh), Hania Smerecka (Archivist, Lloyds Banking Group, Edinburgh) and Irene Swankie (CR & Community Affairs Manager, Clydesdale Bank) for providing additional biographical details of their former employees, Lisa Wood and the staff at Fife Council Archives and Records Management, Markinch, for finding what few school records remain from the Great War, Bill Beveridge (Friends of Kirkcaldy High School) for allowing me sight of his valuable collection of magazines entitled *World War 1914–1919*, Graham A. Ireland (Head of Regulation, Scottish Rugby Union) and John S. Methven (Kirkcaldy RFC) for their excellent contributions on David Howie, and of course, the Rector and office staff at Kirkcaldy High School who allowed me access to the school and the freedom to research the archives undisturbed.

Many organisations provided information on individuals, events, locations, battles and historical facts. The Commonwealth War Graves Commission deserves special mention especially its on-line search facility which provided the necessary information to take my research forward. Special mention, too, must be given to Fife Library Services, especially the librarians at Sinclairtown Library whose help and assistance was freely given no matter how absurd my questions were. Their unfailing good humour and their satisfaction at answering my enquiries helped lighten the burden of my research.

Ryan at Reveille Press deserves thanking. His encouragement and advice was always welcome and constructive especially at those times when I felt I could no longer complete the project.

I must thank my wife, Diana, for the hours she spent assisting me with the production of this book and for assisting with the research, editing and proof reading which brought this project to fruition. Without her support, encouragement and forbearance at my absences from home this book would not have been completed.

Finally, my thanks go to Derek Allan MA Dip Ed FRH, Rector of Kirkcaldy High School, for writing such a moving Foreword.

John S B Beck
Epsom Downs

INTRODUCTION

In the Autumn of 1957, having been successful in passing the 11+ examination I transferred from Dunnikier Primary School to Kirkcaldy High School, then situated in Carlyle Road. I did not realise then that the School had a splendid War Memorial to those teachers and former pupils who fell in the First World War. In 1958 Kirkcaldy High School transferred to a magnificent new building at its present site in Dunnikier Way. For some reason, the Rector, Mr. Robert Adam, decided that the school would be occupied in class order beginning with the second year and that class 2F1 would have the honour of being first to enter. It would be good to record that I was the first pupil to pass through the portals of this new school, but it was not to be and I was fourth to be amazed at this bright, cheerful, purpose built establishment.

I became aware of the School War Memorial, situated in the main entrance hall but, like most of my contemporaries, I ignored it and never really stopped to study the names or even to contemplate why it was there. They were just some folk who had died during the first World War and who had no connection to me. Thus the situation remained until later in life when I became a founder member of the Friends of Kirkcaldy High School whose Committee I eventually joined.

In November 2011, whilst attending a Committee meeting, I noticed that a wreath had been placed at the Memorial and I stopped to look at it. I realised that almost 100 years after the War, these unknown names were being remembered by the school, but who were they? Examination showed that there were teachers and former pupils and that the Memorial bore their name and regiment but nothing else. These men had attended the School and were by assumption from Kirkcaldy or the surrounding district but some had joined, Canadian, Australian, New Zealand, Irish, and other regiments from around the UK not just the Black Watch or the Fife and Forfar Yeomanry. My curiosity was aroused and an idea took shape that perhaps I could flesh out these names with a short biography of each and sell any publication in aid of funds for FoKHS.

Some two years later, I feel I have only scratched the surface but nonetheless have come to know many of these men. Harris Stocks, DSO who was a benefactor to Kirkcaldy and the Boys' Brigade, cousins George and John Lockhart who were in the family linen business, David Methven, the first to be killed in 1914 and John Baldie, the last on 6 November 1918 less than a week before the War's end, Andrew Brown who died in February 1919, and of course the Scottish Rugby international David Dickie Howie and the descendant of Robert Burns, Andrew Currie Begg. The list goes on.

Collecting and researching the information on these local heroes has not been an easy task. The starting point was a surname, initials and regiment. There was no service number, date of birth or death, or any other detail. Furthermore, some of the names were spelled wrongly eg Toogood or Twogood, and some of the records were scant to say the least. Despite this I have tried to say something about everyone on the memorial no matter how elusive they are. I am aware however, that there could be more research waiting to be undertaken to give fuller biographies of these men and I am aware that a second volume could expand on what is already known.

This volume documents briefly the stories of 108 brave sons of Kirkcaldy High School.

KIRKCALDY HIGH SCHOOL – A BRIEF HISTORY

On 10th July 1582 records of Kirkcaldy Burgh show that authority by the Council was given for the establishment of a Burgh School following John Knox's call for every burgh to have a school. Mr. David Spens was appointed first Schoolmaster. He was also a minister of the kirk, setting the precedent for a bond between school and church which lasted for centuries. Indeed the Church was not averse to dictating how the School should be run and insisted that religion played an important part of a boy's education (girls were not thought worthy of education at this time).

The first school was held in a church hall in Kirk Wynd, but five years after its foundation the Council built a new school close to the Church. This sufficed until 1725 when the school was reported to be in ruinous condition and tradesmen of the Burgh demanded that a new school be built. Agreement was reached the same year and construction began on a site in Hill Street near the present 'Fife Free Press' building. In August 1726 the school accepted its first pupils. By 1843 this school had outgrown its usefulness and plans were drawn up by Mr. David Cousin, architect, for a new school to be built in Carlyle Road. This was built to accommodate 300 pupils but it soon became apparent that an extension was necessary. A second storey was added in 1895 and this lasted until the 1960s.

On 20th October 1958 the School left the town centre and moved to its present location at the western corner of Dunnikier Park. It was self-contained with its own playing fields. With the advent of comprehensive education in 1972, the school amalgamated with Templehall Secondary School necessitating further changes to the building. Refurbishment and construction was finally completed in 1994 to provide a school of acknowledged excellence and also to provide social and leisure facilities to the wider community.

Mr. David Spens was the first Schoolmaster and his successors were apparently appointed from within the Burgh until the resignation of

Mr. John Dougall when the Council appointed Mr. Andrew Nevison from another Burgh. He is renowned for two reasons – he held the briefest tenure of office in the School's history (less than a year) and he was the first man to be described as 'Rector'. There have been 18 rectors and during the First World War the post was held by Mr. John D. Rose (1906-1929). He is described as being held in high esteem by staff and pupils alike. He was a classicist and an earnest teacher. His published works included books on teaching English and Religious Education. He took an active part in the life of the community and was prominent in his work with the Boys' Brigade and the local Presbytery. He died in May 1945.

Throughout its history, Kirkcaldy High School was renowned for not just the excellence of its teaching but also for the variety of its extra curricular activities – rugby, hockey, cricket, football, tennis, athletics, netball, swimming, golf, debating, acting, the arts, scouting, guides, chess club, sailing, gliding, music, all designed to equip pupils for adult life.

The School has produced perhaps more than its fair share of successful members of the community – lawyers, teachers, sportsmen, doctors, musicians, indeed all the professions including politics. They have not just settled in the Burgh but have spread throughout the world and have become famous in their adopted countries. It would be difficult to name the most famous of its sons and daughters, but perhaps that honour might be bestowed on Adam Smith, author of *The Wealth of Nations* whose name is commemorated around the town and who was a pupil at the School between 1729 and 1737.

Finally, take a few moments to think of John D. Rose, who knew most of the teachers and former pupils mentioned on the School Memorial. It would have been his sad task to announce their deaths to the school during morning assembly.

(With thanks to John Methven)

PART ONE
THE TEACHERS

JOSEPH SIM HUSBAND

Major Joseph Sim Husband was born in 1889, the son of Arthur Scott Husband and Agnes Barbara Sim Husband, of 147 Logan Street, St Lambert, P.Q., Canada. At the time of his death, his parents were recorded as living in Leven. He is recorded as being a native of Dundee.

Joseph left school and gained a Teaching Certificate from Edinburgh Training College before gaining an MA in English. He began his career as a pupil teacher in Dundee before transferring to Kirkcaldy High School as an English master. He edited the school magazine and took an active interest in all the social and extra scholastic activities of the school. He was a quiet gentlemanly man, a splendid teacher both in scholarship and teaching power.

He was an active church worker and was a member of the Christian Endeavour Society.

At the outbreak of war, he joined up in 1914 as a private soldier in the Gordon Highlanders but was soon selected for officer training and rose to become a Major in the Machine Gun Corps, C Company, 59th Battalion. He was twice Mentioned in Despatches, firstly at Loos and secondly at the capture of Hill 70, for initiative and leadership. He was also awarded the Victory Medal and the British War Medal. His obituary notice in the Fife Free Press claims he was awarded the Military Cross. He was described as a brilliant and daring officer.

Joseph was killed in action on the 11th April 1918 and is buried in grave II.G.2 Pont – d'Achelles Military Cemetery, Nieppe.

JOHN ALEXANDER KING

2nd Lieutenant John Alexander King was a native of Banff where he attended Fordyce Academy and then Aberdeen University graduating with an MA (Hons) in Classics. He migrated to Kirkcaldy where he became a Classics Master at the High School in November 1913. His father was headmaster of Brodiesford School, Fordyce, Banff. John was a married man, having married Miss McCash, a teacher at the High School, in July 1916, whose address was given as Kirkcaldy High School, Carlyle Road, Kirkcaldy. He was described as a man of outstanding ability and of a most cheery and obliging disposition.

He was commissioned on 15th February 1916 in the Gordon Highlanders, 4th Battalion, and saw service in France where he was killed, aged 30 years, by a trench mortar on 12th September 1916. He was awarded the Victory Medal and the British War Medal.

He is buried in grave 11.F.28, Cite Bonjean Military Cemetery, Armentieres. He is also commemorated on Fordyce War Memorial.

THOMAS COLLINS

Lance Corporal Thomas Collins was born in Kilmallie, Inverness-shire and was shown as having an address in Fort William. He became a teacher at the High School and his then current address was shown as Kirkcaldy High School, Carlyle Road, Kirkcaldy. He was the Scoutmaster for the High School Scout troop and was described as a popular and highly esteemed teacher. The High School Log Book records that on 2nd October 1914 "Mr. Thos Collins, a member of staff leaves today for Edinburgh Castle to join the new Edinburgh Battalion for active service." He remained on the staff until August 1916 when a terse log entry states "Mr. Thomas Collins has been killed in action." He was the first of the teachers to volunteer for active service and the first to fall in action. The School magazine of July 1916 noted that his place at school was empty "but his memory lingers, inspiring others with self-sacrifice and patriotic feeling. As a member of the staff he was conscientious and trustworthy, and as a teacher he was deservedly popular." His letters and postcards home were always cheerful and full of interest and he remembered the smallest detail of school life. The article concludes "His influence was ever for good, and his memory will remain ever green."

He joined the 15th Battalion, Royal Scots (Lothian Regiment) in September 1914 but not posted to France until Spring of 1916 where he was promoted to lance corporal. He was awarded the Victory Medal and the British War Medal.

He was killed in action on 1st July 1916 and is commemorated on Pier and Face 6D and 7D of the Thiepval Memorial. His name is also commemorated on the Old Parish Church Memorial and Fort William War Memorial.

PART TWO
THE FORMER PUPILS

HARRIS LAURANCE STOCKS, DSO

Arguably the best known name on the memorial is that of Major Harris Laurance Stocks, DSO, who, aged 45 years, is the oldest of the former pupils to have been killed. He was born on 23rd February 1871 in Kirkcaldy, the second son of Provost John T Stocks, a manufacturer, and his wife Fanny M. Stocks. He had an older brother and sister, Robert and Annie, and two younger sisters, Edith and Fanny.

Harris was educated at Kirkcaldy Burgh School, Cargilfield in Edinburgh and Oliver's Mount School in Scarborough, before spending some time in Switzerland before attending Edinburgh University. On graduating he joined his father's shipping company, the London and Kirkcaldy Shipping Company, which amalgamated with Messrs. Furniss Withy & Co. Ltd. becoming Stocks, Turnbull & Co. Ltd, and eventually HL Stocks Ltd. His address was St. Katherine's, Townsend Crescent, Kirkcaldy.

In 1890 he married Annie F. Balfour, born in 1870 in Edinburgh, daughter of the late Revd. Robert Balfour, DD, a moderator of the Free Church. Annie died in 1906 and their only child died in 1907.

He was an enthusiast in military matters. For many years he was

Captain and later adjutant of the Forth Royal Garrison Artillery Volunteers. He believed in the training of the youth of the Country and was a pioneer of the Boys' Brigade, founded by Sir Alexander Smith. He started the 4th Kirkcaldy Company BB, which was the second largest in Britain with 260 members and a considerable waiting list, in 1893. In 1905 he bought and equipped the Victoria Halls, Victoria Road, Kirkcaldy, for use by the BB which by now had both a brass and a bugle band, and signalling and ambulance sections. An annual camp was held at Rankeillour. He was also interested in the Boy Scout movement and was appointed chairman of the executive Committee of the Scottish Boy Scout Association. In his will he left £25,000 in trust to the Boys' Brigade in Kirkcaldy.

On the outbreak of war, he volunteered and was commissioned as Captain in the Royal Scots, 15th Battalion. He was in the same company as Thomas Collins (qv). On going to France he was promoted temporary Major in October 1914 and substantive Major in January 1915. For bravery in action and devotion to duty, he was awarded the DSO. He also received the Victory Medal and the British War Medal.

He was killed in action on 1st July 1916 and is buried in grave 111.D.11 at Bouzincourt Communal Cemetery Extension. In addition to the School memorial, he is commemorated in Bennochy Cemetery, St. Brycedale Church Memorial Plaque and Kirkcaldy Town War Memorial.

ANDREW CURRIE BEGG

One might be forgiven for believing that a distant relative of Robert Burns would be against any form of war, but not so Captain Andrew Currie Begg who was born at Abbotshall on 13th October 1879, the son of the Revd. Bruce B. Begg, DD, and Mrs. Magdalene Currie Begg, of The Knowe, St. Fillans. He was a descendant of Isabella Burness (27.07.1771 – 04.12.1858) a sister of Robert Burns who had married John Begg.

Andrew attended Kirkcaldy High School and then Edinburgh High School before taking up employment with the Commercial Bank, Kirkcaldy Branch, in May 1896. He subsequently resigned from the Bank to take up a position as a manager with the National Bank of India Ltd., Bishopsgate, London, where he was highly esteemed. He was married to Kate Smith Barber Begg, born in 1881 in the USA, with whom he had six children. Although living in the London area, at the time of his death his address was shown as 68 Milton Road, Kirkcaldy.

Prior to the war, he was a volunteer with the Black Watch and he enlisted in that regiment in November 1914. He was commissioned in March 1915 in the 7th Battalion and in the following November he was promoted to lieutenant and made adjutant. He was also adjutant for the 2nd Inniskillin Fusiliers for the month of December 1915. By a strange irony of fate, he was gazetted captain four days after his death. His colonel wrote of him that "he was a fine soldier and a very gallant and brave man and in the attack on the German trenches on the 30th, seeing men hesitating to go over the parapet, jumped up himself and led them on again and again against hopeless odds. His loss to me will be quite irreplaceable , and I can honestly say it would be almost impossible to find a better adjutant, and in the eight months during which he held that post I had learned not only to value his high qualities as a soldier but to love him as a man." He was awarded the Victory Medal and the British War Medal.

Andrew was killed in action on 30th July 1916 at High Wood. He is buried in grave No. V.G.9 at Serre Road Cemetery No 2 and is commemorated on Abbotshall Parish Church Memorial, St Fillans War Memorial and Kirkcaldy Town Memorial in addition to the School memorial.

EDWARD JAMES BLAIR, MC

Captain Edward James Blair, MC, was one of three brothers who all served in the Royal Army Medical Corps. He was born in 1885, a son of John Blair, a clothier, and Jessie Blair both of Markinch. His mother was the daughter of Mr. & Mrs. Buchan, Glebe Terrace, Alloa.

On leaving school, Edward studied medicine at Edinburgh University, graduating in 1914 as Bachelor of Medicine (MB) and Bachelor of Surgery (ChB). Shortly thereafter he was commissioned in the RAMC and was sent to France where, in 1915 he was wounded by a shell. On return to duty, he continued to serve in France and at the end of 1916 he was awarded the Military Cross for bravery and devotion to duty. He was killed in action whilst going to the relief of a wounded officer.

Edward made the ultimate sacrifice on 11th April 1917and is buried in grave 1V.E.1 at Maroeuil British Cemetery. He is commemorated on Markinch War Memorial.

NORMAN ALEXANDER DOGGART

Captain Norman Alexander Doggart was born in Kirkcaldy in 1891, the youngest of three sons of James M. and Jane K. Doggart of Townsend Cottage, Townsend Place, Kirkcaldy. The family also had connections with St. Andrews and had an address at Abbey Villas there.

Norman excelled at school and was Dux of his year and athletic champion. On leaving the High School he attended Edinburgh University from where he graduated in 1912 with an MA. He then studied medicine for two years until the outbreak of war. He was described as being of manly and staunch character and of pleasant disposition; one of Kirkcaldy's promising young men.

He was Cadet Officer in the school officers training corps and the 'London Gazette' of 29th September 1914 shows that he was appointed 2nd Lieutenant on 23rd September. He joined his regiment, the Cameronians (Scottish Rifles), and in 1915 was sent to France where he remained until 1917 when he was posted to the Bulgarian Front. However, soon thereafter, he transferred to the Royal Air force and was posted to Egypt until July 1918 when he returned to Oxford, England. He was awarded the Victory Medal and the British War Medal.

On 10th October 1918 he died as a result of injuries received in a flying accident. He is buried in grave No. 11.125 at Oxford (Botley) Cemetery. He is commemorated on St. Brycedale Church Plaque and on a memorial stone in St. Andrews Western Cemetery.

FREDERICK HARDIE

Captain Frederick Hardie was born in Dundee, Angus, the son of Mrs. Hardie, latterly of 12 Dalhousie Terrace, Edinburgh. It is not known when the family moved to the Kirkcaldy area, but Frederick attended the High School before studying at Edinburgh University from where he graduated in 1900 as Bachelor of Medicine (MB) and Bachelor of surgery (ChB).

He joined a family doctor practice in Bentham, Lancashire, where he was exceedingly well liked and was described as having a kind and genial disposition. Around 1907, he moved to a practice in Southampton where he remained until joining the army in 1914. He was married to Elsie May Hardie and had two children. At the time of his death, the family home was at 56 Alma Road, Southampton.

Frederick was commissioned as Lieutenant in the Royal Army Medical Corps (Third Wessex (Portsmouth) Field Ambulance) and was promoted Captain six months later. He spent nine months field training in England before being posted to France where he proved himself to be a keen and efficient field ambulance officer. His commanding officer in a letter spoke of Frederick's constant cheeriness and the regard in which he was held by all ranks and added that during his service he had done good work under many dangerous and trying conditions. He was awarded the Victory Medal and the British War Medal.

Frederick was killed on 20th September 1917 and is buried in grave No. 11.A.2 at Trois Arbres Cemetery, Steenwerk. His name is commemorated on Southampton Cenotaph.

FREDERICK WILLIAM HARLEY

Captain Frederick William Harley was born the youngest son of John and Wilhelmina Skirving Harley, Blinkbonny, Kirkcaldy. He attended Kirkcaldy High School, Dollar Academy and George Watson's College in Edinburgh from 1904 to 1906. He then studied engineering and steel manufacture.

On the outbreak of war, he enlisted as a private soldier in the Royal Scots before being commissioned in the 7th Battalion, Black Watch. In June 1915 he was wounded at Festubert and in November he transferred to the Royal Flying Corps (70th Squadron) where he served as an observer before being shot down with his pilot over enemy lines. His fate was confirmed by a message dropped subsequently from a German aircraft. He was awarded the Victory Medal and the British War Medal.

Frederick was killed on 3rd June 1917 and is buried in grave No. 111.A.9/10 in Menen Communal Cemetery. He is also commemorated on St Brycedale Church Memorial Plaque, on the family gravestone in Bennochy Cemetery and on George Watson's College War Memorial.

OSWALD ALEXANDER HERD

Captain Oswald Alexander Herd was born in 1891 in Kirkcaldy, the third son of Peter Herd and Constance EA Grosvenor Herd, of Whytebank, Dunnikier Road, Kirkcaldy. He attended Kirkcaldy High School and George Watson's College, Edinburgh (1906 – 1908) before taking up a position as a mining engineer with the Wemyss Coal Company.

Oswald was gazetted a temporary lieutenant in the Durham Light Infantry on 21st November 1914 and at the time of his death had risen to the rank of captain. He is believed to have been awarded a DSO in addition to the Victory Medal and the British War Medal.

He was killed on 24th September 1916 and is buried in grave No. X11.K.9 at Guards' Cemetery, Lesboefs. He is also commemorated on the Bethelfield Church Memorial plaque and on George Watson's College War Memorial.

GEORGE BARCLAY LOCKHART

Captain George Barclay Lockhart was born in Kirkcaldy in 1893, the son of Barclay Lockhart and Christian Graham Lockhart, of Milton Villa, Milton Road, Kirkcaldy. The family was part of the Lockhart dynasty, well known as linen manufacturers in the town. He was the cousin of Jack Lockhart *(qv)*. George attended the High School and Merchiston Castle School, Edinburgh and on leaving was employed in the family business. He was a member of the Merchiston Castle Officer Training Corps and was a prominent footballer and athlete. He is described as being of a singularly genial disposition.

He was commissioned into the Army Cyclist Corps, Highland Cyclist Battalion (8th (Cyclist Battalion) The Royal Highland Regiment). However, he preferred a faster means of transport and transferred to the Royal Flying Corps until his death when he was shot down and killed. He was awarded the Victory Medal and the British War Medal

He was killed in action on 14th April 1917 and is buried in grave No. V1.D.17 at La Chaudiere Military Cemetery, Vimy. He is commemorated on St. Brycedale Church Memorial Plaque.

WALTER MCFADYEN

Captain Walter McFadyen was born in Kirkcaldy where his parents lived at St. Margaret's, Balwearie Road. He was a distinguished former pupil of the High School and on the outbreak of war was studying analytical chemistry.

He was commissioned into the Royal Scots where he was promoted to captain. He was described as being trusted and loved by his men. He was killed instantly when a shell hit the building he was in some miles from the front when he was on a period of rest and recuperation.

He was killed aged 22 years on 7th May 1917 and is buried in grave No. 1V.G.24 at Faubourg D'Amiens Cemetery, Pas De Calais.

DAVID GEORGE METHVEN

Captain David George Methven was the only son of James and Mary T. Methven of Wemyss Park, Kirkcaldy. He was a former pupil of the High School and, at the age of 35 years, appears to have been a military man since he had seen service in the South African War where he was awarded both the Queen Victoria Medal and the King Edward Medal.

At the outbreak of war he was serving in the 2nd Battalion, Seaforth Highlanders, and was sent to France in August 1914. He was killed near Lille a few weeks later leading his men in a charge against the enemy trenches. His action was described as "heroic" and he was posthumously mentioned in despatches for distinguished bravery. He was awarded the Victory Medal, the British War Medal and the 1914/1915 Star.

David was killed on 20th October 1914 and is buried in grave No. 11.D.19 at Houplines Communal Cemetery Extension. He is commemorated on the family gravestone in Abbotshall Church graveyard and on the Abbotshall Church Memorial Plaque.

IAN COUPER NAIRN

Captain Ian Couper Nairn, MC*, was the only son of John and Gertrude Nairn, of Forth Park, Kirkcaldy, well known linoleum manufacturers. He attended the High School, Cargilfield (Higher Grade) School and Fettes College, Edinburgh. He was an excellent shot, a good all round sportsman and played rugby for Fettes College. On leaving school he travelled extensively in Germany learning about the linoleum industry. On his return to Kirkcaldy he joined the family linoleum business.

He joined the army as a lieutenant in the Fife and Forfar Yeomanry and saw service in Gallipoli, Egypt, Palestine and France. He was awarded the Military Cross and Bar for conspicuous acts of gallantry and devotion to duty in Palestine. At the time of his death he had been promoted to Captain and was serving in the Black Watch, 14th (Fife and Forfar Yeomanry) Battalion. He was well liked by his men and was thoughtful and considerate for their comfort and welfare. In addition to the MC*, he was awarded the Victory Medal and the British War Medal.

His father, John Nairn, donated the library and museum to the Burgh of Kirkcaldy in memory of his son and to those men who gave their lives in the Great War.

Ian was killed on 2nd September 1918 and is buried in grave No. 111.B.35 at Peronne Communal Cemetery Extension. He is also commemorated on a grave stone in Bennochy Cemetery, St Brycedale Church Memorial Plaque and the Town War Memorial.

GILBERT CHISHOLM DREYER SPENCE

Captain Gilbert Chisholm Dreyer Spence, MC, was born in Burntisland, Fife, the son of Dr. Robert and Mrs Annabella Bain Spence. He attended the High School and the Royal Military College, leaving aged 19 on 11th May 1915 having been gazetted a 2nd Lieutenant in the Highland Light Infantry.

Promotion was steady. He was promoted to Lieutenant on 23rd July 1916 and to Captain on 12th August 1917. There is no doubt that he would have risen to higher rank had he not been killed. He was awarded a Military Cross posthumously on 2nd December 1918 for his actions during an engagement with the enemy on 1st October when he showed conspicuous gallantry and able leadership while commanding the support company when the leading companies were held up by enemy machine gun fire. He led his company to high ground which was of vital importance to the rest of the brigade. He was also awarded the Victory Medal and the British War Medal.

He was killed on 1st October 1918 and is buried in grave No. V111.I.11 at Flesquieres Hill British Cemetery. He is also commemorated on Burntisland War Memorial.

WILLIAM ALEXANDER GIBB STEVENSON

Captain William Alexander Gibb Stevenson was born on 14th February 1889, the son of the Revd. William and Mrs. I. W. Stevenson, then of Auchertool and latterly of 4 Kinburn Place, St. Andrews, Fife. He attended the High School and on leaving commenced divinity studies at St. Andrews University. He left university in his third year of studies in 1914 and was commissioned into the 14th (Service) Battalion, Highland Light Infantry.

He was posted to France and saw service in the trenches. He was promoted to captain and was wounded on 25th November 1917 at Cambrai. He was taken prisoner and subsequently died of his wounds in a German hospital. He was mentioned in Sir Douglas Haig's despatches of 22nd December 1917 and was awarded the Victory Medal and the British War Medal.

William died of wounds on 20th December 1917 and is buried in grave 1V.F.13 at Valenciennes (St Roch) Communal Cemetery. His name is commemorated on the Auchertool Parish Church Stained Glass War Memorial.

CHARLES WHITEHEAD YULE

Captain Charles Whitehead Yule, aged 27 years, was the son of James and Thomasina Whitehead Yule, of Strathearn Cottage, Dysart Road, Kirkcaldy. He attended the High School and in 1906 was awarded the Dux Medal. He was also something of a sportsman. On leaving school he attended St. Andrews University where he graduated with a 1st class honours degree in Classics, a 1st class honours degree in Ordinary Logic and a 2nd class honours degree in Humanities. He then became a master at Clifton Bank School before he was nominated by the Secretary of State for Scotland, Lord Pentland, to fill the position of Assistant Curator in the Historical Department of Register House, Edinburgh. He was a member of Carlton Cricket Club, Edinburgh.

On joining the army he was commissioned into the Royal Scots, 13th Battalion, and rose to the rank of Captain. He was recommended for the Military Cross for conspicuous gallantry at Hill 73 and was awarded the Victory Medal and the British War Medal.

He was killed in action on 11th May 1916 and is buried in grave no. 1V.E.5 at Vermelles British cemetery. His name is also recorded on the St. Serf's Church Memorial.

JOHN BOYD BALDIE

Lieutenant John Boyd Baldie was born in Largs, Ayrshire, a son of John and Elizabeth Boyd Baldic, latterly of Royal Bank House, Markinch. John attended the High School, but I have been unable to find out more of his life there. He had a brother, James, who served with the London Scottish Regiment and was killed on 20th May 1915.

However, John answered the call to arms and he joined the Royal Highlanders (Black Watch) as a private in 1914, but at the time of his death he was a lieutenant in the 215th Squadron, Royal Air Force, serving in France. He was shot down and killed just 5 days before the Armistice, so becoming the last former pupil to have been killed in action.

He died on 6th November 1918 and is buried in grave No. 1.D.14 in Charmes Military Cemetery, Essegney. His name is commemorated on Largs War Memorial and Markinch War Memorial.

ROBERT DISHER COUTTS

Lieutenant Robert Disher Coutts was born in 1888, the son of Mr. RA and Mrs. EM Coutts, latterly of 33 Dalhousie Terrace, Edinburgh. Robert attended the High School and then George Watson's College, Edinburgh from 1902 to 1904. He qualified as an accountant and in 1913 was appointed Assistant Auditor in the National Health Insurance Audit Department, Aberdeen.

He was a keen soldier and was a Private in the Territorial Army, 4th Royal Scots. He was gazetted to the Gordon Highlanders in April 1914 and was promoted to Lieutenant, 4th Battalion, in September 1914. On 25th September 1915 he was posted as missing in action at Hooge. It was subsequently established that he had held an isolated position for 16 hours cut off in captured German trenches. He was killed whilst tending wounded colleagues.

He was killed between the 25th and 27th September 1915 and has no known grave. He is remembered on Panel 38 at the Ypres (Menin Gate) Memorial. He is also commemorated on George Watson's College War Memorial.

WILLIAM DARLING DEAS

Lieutenant William Darling Deas was born on 6th January 1888, the only son of William and Thirza D. Deas of Victoria Villa, Victoria Road, Kirkcaldy. His father was a music seller and teacher. William was educated at the High School and George Watson's College, Edinburgh (1902 – 1905) before taking an apprenticeship in February 1905 with the Kirkcaldy Branch of the Bank of Scotland where he was described as smart and intelligent but lacking in application. His uncle was Dr. JS Darling and he was recommended to the Bank by Mr. Bisset, an Agent in the New Town. He resigned from the Bank in February 1908 to take up a position with Messrs John Duncan & Co., London, papermakers. He was soon sent to Canada as their representative but he obtained a position with Messrs M'Farlane, Son & Hodgson, wholesale stationers, in Montreal as their Ontario Traveller. William enjoyed life in Canada and was well known in Montreal. He was Captain of the Montreal Scottish Rugby Club and enjoyed an active social life.

However, on the outbreak of war he was commissioned as a lieutenant into the Argyll and Sutherland Highlanders, 11th Battalion, and by 1915 he was already in France. In early October 1915 he was reported as being wounded but still on duty. The report was later clarified and it became known that he was shot through the leg before being wounded in the head during desperate fighting at Hill 73 near Loos. He is described as being a gallant and capable officer. He was captured by the Germans and was treated at the German Hospital, Wahn, Valenciennes. He was awarded the Victory Medal, the British War Medal and the 1914/15 Star.

William died of wounds on 30th September 1915 and is buried in grave No. 1V.B.10 I Valenciennes (St Roch) Communal Cemetery. His name appears on the George Watson's College War Memorial. He is also commemorated on the family gravestone in Bennochy Cemetery and on the Dunnikier Church memorial.

WILLIAM POLLOCK FRANCIS

Lieutenant William Pollock Francis was born on 30th August 1897, the only son of The Revd. David L. and Mrs. Francis of Raith Manse, Milton Road, Kirkcaldy. He attended the High School where he was a member of the Officers' Training Corps. On leaving School in September 1913 he became an apprentice with Messrs. W. Philip & Son, Engineers where he gained first prize in mechanical engineering.

He enlisted in the Highland Cycle Brigade in February 1915 and on 11th November 1915 he was commissioned into the Royal Scots. He was sent to France and in August 1916 he was wounded by shrapnel during fighting at Messines Ridge. He was sent home to convalesce until 9th October 1916 when he returned to France.

He was killed, aged 20 years, on 22nd October 1917 and is commemorated on Panels 11 to 14 and 162 at Tyne Cot Memorial. He is also commemorated on a gravestone in Abbotshall Churchyard and on the Raith Church Memorial.

He was the third employee of Messrs. Philip & Son to make the ultimate sacrifice.

JAMES SWIRLES HOOD

Lieutenant James Swirles Hood was born on 9th August 1893 at 3 Roseberry Terrace, Kirkcaldy, the son of Andrew and Christine Hood. Andrew had married Christine on 3rd July 1890 in Edinburgh. He was a wine merchant. There were two other sons, Andrew and Roland. By 1911 the family had moved to Harbourhead House, High Street, Kirkcaldy. In 1917, Andrew Hood was a widower and may have had a house in Townsend Place, Kirkcaldy.

James was educated at the High School and then George Watson's College, Edinburgh (1907 – 1909), before joining the Commercial Bank, Pathhead Branch, for some two years. On 4th November 1912 he joined the staff of the head office of the Royal Bank of Canada in Montreal where he remained until enlisting in the

Canadian Expeditionary Force with the 23rd Battalion. At this time, Royal Bank of Canada employees who joined the colours prior to September 1915 were granted leave of absence with an allowance and an understanding that they would be re-engaged after the war. A total of 1,495 members enlisted of whom 186 were killed in action or died of wounds. After training, James was sent to France and at the time of his death he was serving in the 3rd Battalion Canadian Infantry (Central Ontario Regiment). He was awarded the Victory Medal and the British War Medal.

James was killed in action on 3rd May 1917 at Fresnoy. He is buried in grave No. V.C.29 at Orchard Dump Cemetery, Arleux-en-Gohelle. His name is commemorated on a gravestone in Bennochy cemetery and on the Old Parish Church Memorial. His name appears on the George Watson's College War Memorial. He is also commemorated in the Royal Bank of Canada Roll of Honour (published in 1920) and on the Royal Bank of Canada War Memorial (erected 1928) at the Bank's headquarters at 360 St. James Street, Montreal.

JOHN DOUGLAS HUME

Flight Lieutenant John Douglas Hume was born in 1896, the only son of the Revd. David Hume, MA, and Mrs. Florence Stephen Hume, of Muiredge Manse, Buckhaven, Fife. He attended the High School and on leaving took up an engineering apprenticeship with Messrs. Douglas & Grant, Kirkcaldy.

He joined the Royal Navy and was commissioned in the Royal Naval Air Service as a flight sub-lieutenant. He obtained his Aviator's Certificate, No. 1643, on 24th August 1915 and saw service in Mesopotamia. At the time of his death he was attached to HMS President and had been awarded the Distinguished Service Cross.

He died on the 10th December 1916 and is buried in grave No. CC.43 in Sheerness (Isle of Sheppey) Cemetery, Kent. He is also commemorated on Buckhaven War Memorial.

ALEXANDER KILGOUR

Lieutenant Alexander Kilgour was born the second son of Alexander and Mrs Kilgour, Craig Gowan, Loughborough Road, Kirkcaldy. His father was a manufacturer and was Town Treasurer. He attended the High School and on leaving he entered his father's business. He was described as being of a bright, genial disposition.

Alexander joined the Fife and Forfar Yeomanry in 1914 and was commissioned into the Black Watch, 7th Battalion. He saw service in France and was awarded the Victory Medal and the British War Medal.

He was killed in action on 18th April 1918 and is buried in grave No. V.F.8 in Guards Cemetery, Windy Corner, Cuinchy. His name is commemorated on a gravestone in Dysart Cemetery and on the Dunnikier Church Roll of Honour.

JACK SUTHERLAND LOCKHART

THE STRICKEN BRAVE.

THE LATE LIEUT. J. S. LOCKHART.

Lieutenant John (Jack) Sutherland Lockhart was born the younger son of Sir Robert C. and Lady Lockhart, of Allanbank, West Albert Road, Kirkcaldy. Sir Robert, a linen and jute manufacturer, was provost of Kirkcaldy and one of the town's most prominent citizens. He was Sheriff Substitute and was present at the dedication of the town war memorial.

Jack attended the High School and Merchiston Castle School where he played for the rugby 1st XV. On leaving School he joined the family business and took an active part in the social life of the town. He was secretary of Kirkcaldy Rugby Club and represented the Midlands XV against the North of Scotland. He was a member of Kirkcaldy Golf Club. He was a cousin of George Barclay Lockhart *(qv)*.

Jack joined the army soon after the outbreak of war and was commissioned a lieutenant in the Royal Scots, 2nd Battalion. He was twice wounded and was described as being of particularly happy, bright and winsome disposition. He and two others died and three were injured by "a great big air torpedo". He was awarded the Victory Medal and the British War Medal. His death was marked in the town by the flying of flags at half mast on the Town Hall, the YMCA, the High School and the Adam Smith Hall. His promotion to Lieutenant was recorded in the July 1916 High School Magazine (page 61), the same issue that reported his death (page 60)

He was killed on 10th May 1916 and is buried in grave No. 1.B.27 in La Clytte Military Cemetery. His name is commemorated on a gravestone in Bennochy cemetery and on St Brycedale church Plaque.

HARRY MOODIE

Lieutenant Harry Moodie was the youngest son of Mr. & Mrs. HM Moodie of 13 Balsusney Road, Kirkcaldy. He was a brother of Charles Watson Moodie MM who was also killed in action. Harry attended the High School and on leaving was employed in the office of Allen Lithographic Co., Kirkcaldy. He was an active member of the Boys' Brigade and St. Brycedale's Church Sunday School. He was described as being a bright, intelligent young man, full of promise.

Harry was commissioned into the Seaforth Highlanders before transferring to the Royal Air Force, 211 Squadron, as an air gunner. On his last flight over Ostend, he shot down two enemy aircraft before being attacked by a German plane. His pilot managed to return to the airfield but it was found that a bullet had entered Harry's back, through a lung and exited through his chest. Harry died from extensive internal bleeding. He was described as being one of the finest officers the RAF ever had, the very best of men.

Harry died on 16th September 1918 aged 20 years and is buried in grave No. 1V.C.18 in Dunkirk Town Cemetery. He is commemorated on the St. Brycedale Church Memorial Plaque.

ALEXANDER ROBERTSON

Lieutenant Alexander Robertson was the eldest son of Mr. WJ and Mrs. Robertson of Seaview, Dysart. He attended the High School and on leaving was employed there as a laboratory assistant. He had been a member of the Officer Training Corps and it had been his intention to study for the medical profession.

However, in October 1915 he enlisted in the Royal Field Artillery prior to his transfer to the Royal Flying Corps, 34th Squadron. He was on observation duty at an altitude of 3,500 feet when he was struck on the left hand side by rifle fire from the ground. He was 21 years old. He was awarded the Victory Medal and the British War Medal.

He died on 17th August 1917. Alexander is buried in grave No. 1.A.4 at Zuydcoote Military Cemetery. His name is commemorated on Dysart War Memorial, on a gravestone in Dysart Cemetery and on St. Serfs Church Memorial Plaque.

JAMES M. WALLACE

Lieutenant James Miller Wallace was born on 8th June 1888 the son of Alexander and Jeannie Wallace, latterly of 20 Forth Avenue North, Kirkcaldy. Alexander pre-deceased his son. James attended the High School where he took many prizes in studies and athletics. The School magazine of June 1908 (page 58) records that he attended St Andrews University where he "gained 2nd place in 1st rank in Ordinary History; gained special prize for essays in ordinary history; gained 2nd place in 1st rank in honours in Political Economy; gained 5th place in 2nd rank in ordinary French". He graduated in 1911 with an MA degree. On leaving, he emigrated to Canada where he settled in Manitoba, becoming principal of Swan River High School from 1914 to 1916.

He was commissioned into the Canadian Expeditionary Force, 43rd Battalion Canadian Infantry (Manitoba Regiment) which had been formed in late 1916. He was sent to France where he saw action. He was awarded the Victory Medal and the British War Medal.

James was killed in action on 27th August 1918 aged 30 years and is buried in grave No. 11.B.28 in Windmill British Cemetery, Monchy-Le-Preux. His name is commemorated on a gravestone in Bennochy Cemetery and Raith Church Memorial. His name is also recorded in the Canadian Virtual War Memorial, and the Canadian Roll of Honour in the Peace Tower, Ottawa.

ROBERT ANDERSON

2nd Lieutenant Robert Anderson was the son of James and Margaret Anderson of Inchview, Lady Nairn Avenue, Kirkcaldy. On leaving the High School, Robert, known as Bert, was employed in the offices of Michael Nairn & Co., Kirkcaldy.

He was commissioned into the Royal Scots, 2nd Battalion, and sent to France. When news of his death arrived, his mother was a patient in Edinburgh Royal Infirmary where she died a few days later.

Aged 24, Robert died of his wounds on 23rd March 1918 at no. 43 Casualty Clearing Station and is buried in grave No. 1.A.24 at Bac-du-Sud British Cemetery, Bailleulval. His name is commemorated on a gravestone in Dysart Cemetery.

JAMES HOWIESON BARNET

2nd Lieutenant James Howieson Barnet was born the older son of Alexander and Eliza Jane Howieson Barnet of Meadowbank, West Albert Road, Kirkcaldy. On leaving the High School he joined the family business, Barnet & Morton, Ironmongers, Kirkcaldy. He sang in the Victoria Road Church Choir and was a Sunday School Teacher. He was Secretary of Kirkcaldy Tennis Club. In June 1917, James married Margaret Rutherford Sinclair, of Linwood, Cathcart, Glasgow. His younger brother, Henry Morton Barnet *(qv)* also died on active service.

James enlisted on 1st May 1916 and was commissioned into the Black Watch (Royal Highlanders) 4th Battalion and was sent to France. He was awarded the Victory Medal and the British War Medal.

On 1st August 1918, aged 31 years, he was killed in action and is buried in grave No. 111.E.5 in Raperie British Cemetery, Villemontoire. His name is commemorated on a gravestone in Bennochy Cemetery and in St. Andrews Church Memorial.

HENRY MORTON BARNET

2nd Lieutenant Henry Morton Barnet was born the youngest son of Alexander and Eliza Jane Howieson Barnet, of Meadowbank, West Albert Road, Kirkcaldy. On leaving the High School, Henry attended George Watson's College, Edinburgh. He was then employed by Messrs Brown, M'Farlane & Co., Glasgow. His older Brother, James Howieson Barnet *(qv)* was killed in action during the war.

He was commissioned into the King's Royal Rifle Corps, 1st Battalion, as a 2nd Lieutenant. He was wounded and taken prisoner on 24th March 1917 when he was transferred to Ohrdruf, Saxony. He was awarded the Victory Medal and the British War Medal.

Henry died of wounds, aged 27, on 23rd April 1918 and is buried in grave No. 1V.E.12 at Niederzwehren Cemetery. His name is commemorated on a gravestone in Bennochy Cemetery and on St Andrews Church Memorial.

BEAUMONT CROWTHER OSWALD BEATSON

2nd Lieutenant Beaumont Crowther Oswald Beatson, was born the only son of Mr. and Mrs. David Oswald Beatson of Townsend Place, Kirkcaldy. His father was born in 1864 in Kirkcaldy and was a wine merchant. Beaumont was educated at the High School and Sedbergh School before working in his father's business.

He enlisted in the Royal Scots but in August 1915 he obtained a commission in the Black Watch, 7th Battalion. He was sent to France and saw active service during which he was twice wounded. He was awarded the Victory Medal and the British War Medal.

He was killed in action on 23rd April 1917 and is buried in grave No. 11.H.23 in Brown's Copse Cemetery, Roeux. His name is commemorated on a gravestone in Bennochy Cemetery and on St Peter's Church Memorial.

ANDREW ROBERTSON BELL

2nd Lieutenant Andrew Robertson Bell was the eldest son of Mr. John L. and Mrs. Jane Eliza Robertson Bell, of 19 David Street, Kirkcaldy. John L. Bell was headmaster of Abbotshall Public School. On leaving the High School, Andrew began training as an analytical chemist with Barry Ostlere & Shepherd Ltd but in June 1917 he was commissioned in to the Royal Flying Corps.

After training, he was sent to Italy and whilst there he was involved in a flying accident which proved fatal. He had been testing an improved engine in an aeroplane when he crashed. He was one of the youngest of the former pupils to have lost his life and at the time of his death the family appears to have been living at Craiglea, Abbotshall Road, Kirkcaldy. He was awarded the Victory Medal and the British War Medal.

Andrew died, aged 19 years, on 22nd September 1918 and is buried in plot 5 row B grave 3 at Montecchio Precalcino Communal Cemetery Extension. His name is commemorated on St Brycedale Church Memorial.

JAMES BURT

2nd Lieutenant James Burt was the eldest son of James and Margaret L. Burt, 184 High Street, Kirkcaldy. James Burt, (father) was a bookseller and stationer and the business continued well into modern times. James (son) was awarded a medal for English literature whilst at the High School and was looking to a literary career when he joined up. He played the violin and was platoon sergeant in the High School Cadet Corps. He was a member of St Brycedale's Church, superintendent of the Children's League of Worship and secretary of the minister's bible class.

In March 1917 he was commissioned into the Black Watch, 3rd Battalion, and was sent to France. He turned down an offer from a daily paper to write articles from the Front. He had been transferred to the 8th Battalion and at the time of his death he was leading his men in an attack on Meteren, France. He was reported to have combined firmness with courtesy. He was awarded the Victory Medal and the British War Medal.

James was killed in action aged 20 years, on 19th July 1918 and is buried in grave No. 11.B. 87 in Meteren Military Cemetery. His name is commemorated on a gravestone in Abbotshall Churchyard and on St Brycedale Church Memorial Plaque.

GILMOUR CUMMING

2nd Lieutenant Gilmour Cumming was the son of Alexander and Margaret Cumming, of 35 High Street, Leven, Fife. He attended the High School where he was described as being a good and steady lad in school.

He was commissioned, aged 18 years and straight from school, into the Black Watch, 5th Battalion and was sent to France. At some stage he transferred to the 1st/7th Battalion. Page 61 of the School magazine of July 1916 records that he was one of six pupils who enlisted during Session 1915-1916. He met his death in a peculiarly gallant manner, being surrounded by Germans he fought to the last. A letter from a Corporal Laird to the Rector of the High School gave a graphic account of Gilmour's death and confirmed that he had in fact been surrounded by the enemy before succumbing. "He was one of the finest officers and as brave a chap as ever fired a rifle." He was awarded the Victory Medal and the British War Medal.

Gilmour was killed in action aged 20 years on 21st March 1918. He is commemorated on Bay 6 of the Arras Memorial.

PETER GODFREY DELAHUNT

2nd Lieutenant Peter Godfrey Delahunt proved to be one of the more difficult former pupils to identify not least because he is known simply as "Godfrey Delahunt" on the school memorial. He was born Peter Godfrey on 1st July 1898 in Lauder, Berwickshire, the youngest son of Peter and Maria Helen Knapman Delahunt. He was affectionately known as "Patsy". He also had a sister called Alice. The family had an address at 92 Dunnikier Road, Kirkcaldy although Peter (son) is recorded as being a native of Kinghorn and his father is reported to have been a Kinghorn Town Councillor.

The Supplement to the London Gazette shows that Peter was commissioned into the Black Watch in November 1917 and he was posted to the 4th Battalion. He was sent to France where he saw action. He was awarded the Victory Medal and the British War Medal.

He died of wounds, aged 20 years, on 28th August 1918 at 33 Casualty Clearing Station, Ligny, Pas de Calais, France, and is buried in grave No.11.E.3 at Ligny-St Flochel British Cemetery. He is commemorated on Kinghorn Town War Memorial.

WILLIAM GIBSON

2nd Lieutenant William Gibson was born the eldest son of William and Alison Gibson, 12 Macduff Crescent, Kinghorn. William attended Kinghorn Public School prior to Kirkcaldy High School. On leaving he studied law at Edinburgh University. He was a recognised athlete. His father was a Bailie (Justice of the Peace or Magistrate).

William was commissioned in to the 14th Battalion Royal Scots and at the time of his death aged 21 he was serving with the 15th Battalion. He was awarded the Victory Medal and the British War Medal.

He was killed on 1st July 1916, the first day of the battle of the Somme. He has no known grave and is commemorated on Pier and Face 6D and 7D of the Thiepval Memorial. He is also commemorated on Kinghorn Town War Memorial.

GEORGE B. HENDERSON

2nd Lieutenant George Ballingall Henderson was born on 12th April 1893 the son of Robert and Margaret Henderson then of 18 Russell Place, Kirkcaldy. Robert was a sculptor by trade and he predeceased his son. Margaret subsequently moved to 9 West Albert Road, Kirkcaldy. George attended the High School but little is known of his time there.

The London Gazette of 9th March 1917 reports that he was commissioned into the Machine Gun Corps

He was killed on 31st October 1918, just a few days before the Armistice and unusually, is buried in grave No. A.33 in Kirkcaldy (Bennochy) Cemetery. His name does not appear on Kirkcaldy War Memorial under the Machine Gun Corps entry, but he is commemorated as George Ballingham Henderson in the Scottish Roll of Honour at the Scottish National War Memorial, Edinburgh Castle.

DAVID DICKIE HOWIE

2nd Lieutenant David Dickie Howie was born on 12th May 1888 in Roseberry Temple, Midlothian, the son of Archibald and Jessie Howie of The Grange, Kinghorn, Fife. The family were farmers and David attended the High School where he excelled at sports, especially rugby, playing as a lock forward.

On leaving school, he continued his interest in rugby, playing locally for Kirkcaldy Rugby Club and such was his expertise he was capped for Scotland on five occasions in 1912 against France, Wales, Ireland, England and South Africa, and twice in 1913 against France and Wales. His half brother, Robert Howie, also played for Scotland on seven occasions and was part of the Scottish team in its first ever Grand Slam win in 1925. Robert toured South Africa with the British Lions in 1924. Robert used to tell a story that he had to look after David's horse while David played for Kirkcaldy in the Beveridge Park. Their father disapproved of their playing rugby and there is a quote of him saying "Rugby an' fermin' will no agree, an' A ken which'll pit mair money in yer pooch".

David found time to take a wife and in 1914 he married Marie Winifred Linton, daughter of Dr. Linton, Edinburgh, in Kinghorn. At the time of his death they were living at 1 Mayfield Gardens, Edinburgh.

David was commissioned into the Royal Field Artillery, 2nd Highland Brigade, and was eventually sent to Gallipoli where he contracted a tropical disease and was evacuated to a hospital in Cairo, Egypt. He was awarded the Victory Medal and the British War Medal.

David died of malaria on 19th January 1916 in Cairo. He is buried in grave no D.267 in Cairo War Memorial Cemetery. His name is commemorated on Kinghorn War Memorial. The Scottish RFU War Memorial Arch at Murrayfield bears no names but commemorates in general the 30 Scottish International Players who died in both World Wars.

JAMES HERBERT LOCKHART

2nd Lieutenant James Herbert Lockhart was born the youngest son of James Peddie Lockhart and Mary Cox Hutchison Lockhart, of the Elms, Nicol Street, Kirkcaldy. He attended the High School where he was a keen sportsman, playing cricket for the school. He became a member of Kirkcaldy Cricket Club. On leaving school, he became an apprentice engineer with Messrs Sang, CE, and on qualifying as a civil engineer he went to India, aged 20 years. He later worked for some 10 years on the construction of the Aswan (Assuam *sic)* Dam.

James returned to the UK and was commissioned into the Black Watch, 7th Battalion, and was sent to France where he took part in the Somme Offensive. He was awarded the Victory Medal and the British War Medal.

He was killed, aged 32 years, on 30th July 1916 and is buried in grave No. 1V.A.11 in Combles Communal Cemetery Extension. His name is also commemorated on a gravestone in Abbotshall Churchyard and on the Abbotshall Church Memorial.

JOHN WILLIAM MUSGROVE

2nd Lieutenant John William Musgrove was born the son of William and Mary Emily Musgrove, 93 Victoria Road, Kirkcaldy. John attended the High School and left aged 17years to enlist on the first day of War.

He was commissioned in to the Black Watch, 4th Battalion and served in Gallipoli, Egypt and France. John's father predeceased him. Having served from the beginning it is sad that John died less than four months from the end of hostilities. He was awarded the Victory Medal and the British War Medal.

John was killed, aged 21 years, on 19th July 1918. He is buried in grave No. 11.J.247 in Meteren Military Cemetery. He is also commemorated on Kirkcaldy Old Parish Church Memorial.

JAMES MF REILLY

2nd Lieutenant James MF Reilly was born the son of Mr. and Mrs. John Reilly, of 6 Roseberry Terrace, Kirkcaldy. James attended the High School and was studying as a junior student with the intention of becoming a teacher. He was good at English and history was his favourite subject. He was a member of High School's Officer Training Corps.

He enlisted in March 1916 aged 19 years and was commissioned into the Royal Scots, which event was noted in the July 1916 issue of the school magazine. He was sent to France and during the winter of 1916 he was wounded in the foot. He was awarded the Victory Medal and the British War Medal.

James was killed in action aged 20 years on 20th September 1917. He has no known grave and is commemorated on the Tyne Cot Memorial, Panel 11 to 14 and 162.

ALBERT JOHN ROBERTSON

Sub-lieutenant Albert John Robertson was the only son of Duncan and Mrs. Robertson of 19 Sang Road, Kirkcaldy. He attended the High School and on leaving he was employed by John Connell and Sons, Shipping Agent. He played cricket and football. The family moved to 21 Stanley Street, Rosyth.

He was commissioned into the Royal Naval Volunteer Reserve in August 1917 and was attached to Nelson Battalion, Royal Naval Division on 1st January 1918. He was sent to France and was being taken to hospital with an injured heel when the ambulance in which he was travelling was hit by shell fire. He was taken to the 149th (RN) Field Ambulance for treatment.

The impersonal nature of War is highlighted when one reads the reason for Albert's death. His service record simply reads "Discharged Dead".

Albert died of wounds on 4th January 1918 aged 20 years and is buried at Thiepval Memorial (MR21). His name is commemorated on St Brycedale Church Memorial.

PERCY KIRK SMITH

2nd Lieutenant Percy Kirk Smith was born the only son of Mr. & Mrs. Thomas Smith, 'Westerlea', Swan Road, Kirkcaldy. He attended the High School and then studied at Heriott Watt College in Edinburgh. He served an apprenticeship with Messrs Philip & Son, Kirkcaldy, prior to taking up a position in the drawing office of the Lochgelly Coal and Iron Company.

Percy was commissioned in to the Royal Engineers, 212th Field Company, in February 1917 and was sent to France. He was awarded the Victory Medal and the British War Medal.

He was killed on 12th September 1917 aged 26 years and is buried in grave No. 111.R.5 in Ridge Wood Military Cemetery. He is commemorated on a gravestone in Bennochy cemetery and on St Brycedale Memorial Plaque.

GEORGE GRIEVE SWAN

2nd Lieutenant George Grieve Swan was born the son of Mr. & Mrs. T. Swan, Annfield, Milton Road, Kirkcaldy. He attended the High School where he was a member of the cadet corps and on leaving took up an apprenticeship as a civil engineer with W. Lockhart, Kirkcaldy. On qualifying, he took up a position with the North British Railway. He was a cousin of George Harry Swan *(qv)*.

George was commissioned into the Manchester Regiment, 4th Battalion, in May 1915 and in December 1915 his rank was substantiated and he was transferred to the 22nd Battalion. In May 1916 he was sent to France where he took part in the battle of the Somme. He was awarded the Victory Medal and the British War Medal.

George was killed on 1st July 1916, the first day of the battle of the Somme, aged 27 years barely a month after his arrival in France. He has no known grave but his name is commemorated on the Thiepval Memorial, Pier and Face 13A and 14C. He is also commemorated on the West End Congregational Church Memorial and the North British Railway Memorial, Waverley Station, Edinburgh.

GEORGE HARRY SWAN

2nd Lieutenant George Harry Swan was born the son of George and Maggie Swan, 12 West Albert Road, Kirkcaldy. He attended the High School and George Watson's College, Edinburgh, from 1909 to 1913 before attending Edinburgh University where he began studying for a Bachelor of Science degree in chemistry. He was described as being a successful student and of excellent character. He was a cousin of George Grieve Swan *(qv)*.

George was commissioned into the Royal Scots Fusiliers, 9th Battalion, on 16th August 1915 and later transferred to the 1st Battalion. He was sent to France and was involved in the heavy fighting on the Somme. He was awarded the Victory Medal and the British War Medal.

He was killed in action aged 21 years on 14th July 1916, two weeks after his cousin. George has no known grave but is mentioned on Special Memorial 7 in Flatiron Copse Cemetery, Mametz. He is also commemorated on a gravestone in Bennochy Cemetery and West End Congregational Church Memorial. His name appears in George Watson's College Roll of Honour and War Memorial.

FRANK FAIRWEATHER WATSON

2nd Lieutenant Frank Fairweather Watson was born a son of Forbes and Louisa Fairweather Watson of 18 Grindlay Street, Edinburgh. He attended the High School and Edinburgh University which he represented at both rugby and football. He was the brother of Sidney Fairweather Watson *(qv).* His mother received a letter from Frank saying he was safe and well just one hour before she received a telegram informing her that he had been killed. His father predeceased him and at the time of his death his mother was living at Thornliebank, Forth Street, Dysart.

Frank was commissioned into the Royal Scots, 14th Battalion, on 24th February 1915 and became an expert signaller to such an extent that he trained fellow officers to be signallers. He was highly esteemed and at the time of his death he was attached to the 15th Battalion. He was awarded the Victory Medal and the British War Medal.

He was killed in action on 4th August 1916 aged 23 years and is buried in grave No. XV1.D.20 in Caterpillar Valley Cemetery, Longueval. His name is commemorated on Barony Church Plaque and on Dysart War Memorial.

SIDNEY FAIRWEATHER WATSON

2nd Lieutenant Sidney Fairweather Watson was the younger son of Forbes and Louisa Fairweather Watson of 18 Grindlay Street, Edinburgh. He was educated at the High School before leaving to become a law clerk with Messrs. J. & J. L. Innes, Kirkcaldy. He was the brother of Frank Fairweather Watson *(qv)* who predeceased him by some six weeks. His father had also predeceased him and his mother was living at Thornliebank, Forth Street, Dysart.

Sidney enlisted at the age of 18 years in September 1914 and was commissioned into the Gordon Highlanders, 2nd Battalion, in May 1915. The School magazine of December 1914 notes that he had enlisted as a bugler in H Company, 4th Battalion, Royal Scots. He saw service in France and took part in the Somme offensive. He was awarded the Victory Medal and the British War Medal.

Sidney was killed in action on 6th September 1916 aged 20 years and has no known grave. He is commemorated on the Thiepval Memorial, Pier and Face 15B and 15C. He is also commemorated on Barony Church Memorial and Dysart War Memorial.

DAVID JOHN WHITTON

Surgeon Probationer David John Whitton, was the only son of William and Mrs. Whitton of St. Clair Street, Kirkcaldy. He attended Dunnikier Primary School before transferring to the High School. He then went on to Edinburgh University to study medicine. He was in his third year as a medical student when he was appointed junior house surgeon to Professor Alexis Thomson at Edinburgh Royal Infirmary. Soon after he was offered the post of senior house surgeon, but he declined the offer to join the navy. He was not an outdoor type of person preferring to play the violin. He was described as having an exceedingly attractive personality.

David was commissioned in to the Royal Naval Volunteer Reserve and was serving on board HMS Cullist – previously cargo steamship Q-ship Westphalia – in Dundalk Bay when it was torpedoed and sunk by German submarine U97.

He was killed in action on 11th February 1918, aged 21 years, and was lost at sea. He is commemorated on Portsmouth Naval Memorial. His name is also commemorated on a gravestone in Bennochy Cemetery and on St. Brycedale Church Memorial.

GEORGE BOAK LANG

Sergeant George Boak Lang, MM, was born on 16th March 1894 at 366 High Street, Kirkcaldy, the son of Arthur and Agnes Boak Lang. Arthur was a retired farmer who predeceased his son. His mother then lived at 110 Dunnikier Road, Kirkcaldy. George attended the High School but I have found little about his time there.

He enlisted in the Royal Engineers and rose through the ranks to become a Sergeant in the 93rd Field Company. The December 1914 School magazine records that George enlisted as a sapper. He saw action in France and was awarded the Military Medal for gallantry. He was also awarded the Victory Medal and the British War Medal.

George was killed in action at Cambrai on 14th October 1918 aged 24 years, just a few weeks prior to the Armistice, and is buried in grave No. 11.F.7 at Caudry British Cemetery, Nord Pas de Calais. He is also commemorated on a gravestone in Bennochy Cemetery.

NORMAN MCLEOD BROWN

Sergeant Norman McLeod Brown was born the son of Mr. and Mrs. Robert Brown, 70 High Street, Kirkcaldy. His father was a draper at that address and it is of note that the premises are now occupied by NB Clothing Shop. Norman attended the High School and on leaving he went to London where he obtained an important appointment in the India Office.

On the outbreak of war, he enlisted in to the London Regiment (London Scottish) C Company, 1st/14th Battalion. The 1st Battalion was the first Territorial force to go into battle and arrived there from Calais in 34 London Transport buses. At the time of his death he had been recommended for a commission. He was the third former High School pupil to have been killed with the London Scottish Regiment. It is of note that he was killed the day before the famous "Christmas Truce" took place. He was eligible for the award of the Victory Medal, the British War Medal and the 1914/15 Star.

Norman was killed in action on 24th December 1914 aged 27 years and is buried in grave No. 111.N.29 at Arras Road Cemetery, Roclincourt, Pas de Calais. He is also commemorated on a gravestone in Bennochy Cemetery and the London Scottish Regiment War Memorial, Horseferry Road, London, SW1

JOHN S. CRUTCHLOW

Sergeant John Stewart Crutchlow was the son of George and Elizabeth Crutchlow. His father predeceased him and his mother is recorded as being known as Elizabeth McIlroy of 6 John Street, Kirkcaldy. At the time of his death his mother was living at Mayview, Windmill Road, Dysart. John attended the High School where he was a member of the Cadet Corps and on leaving became an apprentice pattern maker with Messrs. Douglas & Grant, engineers. He was described as a man of soldierly bearing and was well known and respected.

In 1911 he enlisted in the Army Cyclist Corps, 52nd (Lowland) Division, Cyclist Company and rose through the ranks to become a Sergeant. His rank and name are recorded on page 13 of the December 1914 School magazine. He was eventually posted to Egypt. He was awarded the Victory Medal and the British War Medal.

John was killed in action aged 20 years on 4th August 1916 in Egypt. He is buried in grave No.E.237 at Kantara War Memorial Cemetery, Egypt. He is also commemorated on a gravestone in Dysart Cemetery and on Galatown Church Roll of Honour.

WALTER BAILIE HONEYMAN

Sergeant Walter Bailie Honeyman was born the second son of Archibald P. and Flora C. Honeyman. His father, a solicitor, predeceased him and at the time of Walter's death, his mother was living at 7 Killeen Road, Rathmines, Co. Dublin. Walter attended the High School but little is known of his early life. He was a grandson of the Very Revd. Dr. Johnston, Dean of St. Andrews. He was one of the oldest of the former pupils to have made the ultimate sacrifice.

He enlisted in the Royal Dublin Fusiliers, 7th Battalion, and attained some promotion – Sergeant according to the school memorial, lance corporal according to the Commonwealth War Graves Commission. At some time he transferred to the Labour Corps, 962nd Area Employment Company. The Labour Corps was formed in January 1917 with men no longer fit for front-line service. Their cap badge comprised in brass, a rifle, shovel and pick piled together with the motto *Labor Omnia vincit* (Work conquers all). Towards the end of the war Walter found himself in Italy.

On 13th October 1918, aged 39 years, he died of pneumonia in an Italian hospital and he is buried in grave No. 1V.A.8 at Taranto Town Cemetery Extension. He is also commemorated on Holy Trinity Church Memorial, Rathmines, and on St. Peters Church Memorial.

JOHN LEITCH

Sergeant John Leitch was born the son of Henry and Jessie Leitch, 37 Balfour Street, Kirkcaldy. He attended the High School and on leaving went to college as a junior student with the aim of qualifying as a teacher.

Whilst still a teenager, John enlisted in the Black Watch, 7th Battalion, as a private. The school memorial shows him to be a sergeant, but Commonwealth War Grave records show him to be a private at the time of his death. He was awarded the Victory Medal and the British War Medal.

John was killed in action, aged 20 years, on 28th July 1916 and is buried in grave No. 1.L.53 at Albert Communal Cemetery Extension. He is also commemorated on a gravestone in Bennochy Cemetery.

WILLIAM SINCLAIR MILLER

Sergeant William Sinclair Miller was born 19th July 1897, the only son of John and Mrs Miller. He attended the High School and on leaving, still in his teens, he emigrated to Canada.

He enlisted as a private in the Canadian Infantry (Quebec Regiment) 14th Battalion and according to the school memorial, he attained the rank of sergeant. However, the Canadian Great War Project and the Commonwealth War Graves Commission show him to be a private at the time of his death. He was awarded the Victory Medal and the British War Medal.

William died of wounds on 9th October 1917, aged 20 years, and is buried in grave No. 11.D.42 in Barlin Communal Cemetery Extension. His name is also commemorated on page 294 of the Canadian Virtual War Memorial.

RICHARD OLIVER

Sergeant Richard Oliver was the only son of Richard and Jeanie Oliver, 349 High Street, Kirkcaldy. Richard had one sister and his father was a butcher. The shop is currently a chemist's shop. He attended the High School and was described as having a bright happy disposition.

He enlisted in the Black Watch, 14th (Fife and Forfar Yeomanry) Battalion and according to Commonwealth War Graves Commission records he had attained the rank of Lance Sergeant at the time of his death. Page 13 of the December 1914 School magazine notes that he was a Lance Corporal in the Fife and Forfar Yeomanry. He saw active service and had been posted to Egypt. He was awarded the Victory Medal and the British War Medal.

William was killed on 28th December 1917, aged 26 years, and is buried in grave No. Y.82 at Jerusalem War Cemetery. He is commemorated on two gravestones, in Abbotshall Churchyard and Bennochy Cemetery.

ARTHUR STANLEY REID

Sergeant Arthur Stanley Reid was born in 1885 in Dunfermline, the son of Henry and Mary MSD Reid, later of 4 Swan Road, Kirkcaldy. He had a sister called Frances Eliza. He attended the High School where he excelled at athletics and was Cadet Sergeant in the Cadet Corps. On leaving school he studied Arts at Edinburgh University between 1903 and 1907 and graduated with 1st class MA (Hons) in Classics. He took up teaching as a career and became Classics Master at Motherwell Higher Grade School.

Arthur enlisted in October 1914 as a private in the Royal Scots, (Lothian Regiment) 15th Battalion and by December 1915 he had been promoted to Sergeant and sent to France. He was awarded the Victory Medal and the British War Medal.

He was killed in action on 1st July 1916, aged 31 years, near Albert and has no known grave. His name is commemorated on Pier and Face 6D and 7D of the Thiepval Memorial. He is also commemorated on a gravestone in Bennochy Cemetery, on Bethelfield Church Plaque and on Motherwell War Memorial.

THOMAS SMITH

Sergeant Thomas Smith was born the son of Thomas & Grace Brown Wilkie Smith, Manuel Cottage, Dunnikier Road, Kirkcaldy. He attended the High School and after leaving was employed as a draughtsman with Melville Brodie Engineering Company, Kirkcaldy. He is described as being of a genial, cheery disposition and a most likeable lad. It is reported that the flags at Starks Park (home of Raith Rovers Football Club) were flown at half mast in his honour when his death became known. I have been unable to find his connection with Starks Park.

He enlisted in the Royal Engineers, 1st Field Survey Company, and was promoted to Sergeant and sent to France. He was awarded the Victory Medal and the British War Medal.

Thomas died aged 24 years on 15th April 1918 from gas poisoning and wounds received. He is buried in grave No. 1.F.20 in Houchin British Cemetery. His name is commemorated on a gravestone in Bennochy Cemetery and on the Union Church Plaque.

ALEXANDER THOMSON LESSLIE CURROR

Corporal Alexander Thomson Lesslie Curror was born on 19th May 1891 in Kirkcaldy, the son of Peter and Marion Curror of Newton House, Nicol Street, Kirkcaldy. He attended the High School where he was called Sandy and was a moderately successful athlete. The School magazine of December 1908 records on page 12 that he was appointed one of three signallers in the School OTC. After leaving he was registered as a temporary boy clerk in the Civil Service on 23rd January 1907 (The Edinburgh Gazette, 5th February 1907). However, this work did not suit him and he eventually emigrated to Canada where he took up farming at Banchory Farm, Elstow, Saskatchewan. He never married despite being a good looking young man – fair complexion, blue eyes, light brown hair, above average height and very fit.

Alexander enlisted in the Canadian Infantry (British Columbia Regiment) 72nd Battalion on 8th March 1916 and agreed to serve overseas. He was sent to France and he was promoted to corporal. He saw active service and was awarded the Victory Medal and the British War Medal.

Alexander was killed on 1st March 1917 aged 25years, and he was buried in grave No. X11.F.5 in Cabaret-Rouge British Cemetery, Souchez. His name is also commemorated in the Canadian Virtual War Memorial, the Canadian National Roll of Honour, page 224, and on Saskatchewan War Memorial.

ALEXANDER DUNSIRE

Private Alexander Dunsire was born in Kinghorn, the eldest son of Thomas and Jessie Dunsire. Alexander was affectionately known as Sandy. He had three brothers. His father predeceased him and his mother lived at 15 Sang Place, Kirkcaldy. He attended the High School and on leaving in May 1908 he took up an apprenticeship with the Royal Bank of Scotland, Kirkcaldy Branch. He moved to the London office of the bank in March 1913 but in May 1913 he resigned to enlist in the army.

He joined the Royal Scots and at the time of his death was serving as a private in the 11th Battalion. He was awarded the Victory Medal and the British War Medal.

Alexander died of wounds at 13 Casualty Clearing Station aged 26 years, on 20th August 1918 and is buried in grave No. V.D.75 in Longuenesse (St Omer) Souvenir Cemetery. His name is commemorated on a gravestone in Kinghorn Cemetery but he is not commemorated on the town War Memorial.

ROBERT FYFE

Corporal Robert Fyfe was born in Marylebone, London, in 1897, the son of Robert and Euphemia Fyfe later of 20 Ava Street, Kirkcaldy. His father was a plumber. He attended the High School and on leaving was employed by the British Linen Bank, Kirkcaldy Branch.

Robert enlisted whilst a teenager in to the Royal Scots Fusiliers, 1st/4th Battalion and was soon promoted to corporal. He was awarded the Victory Medal and the British War Medal.

On 15th April 1917 Robert was one of a number of replacement troops being sent to Egypt when the transport ship, HT Arcadian, was torpedoed 26miles northeast of Melos by German submarine UC74 captained by Kapitainleutnant Wilhelm Marschall. Robert, who was only 20years old, was one of the 277 persons who lost their lives during the six minutes it took for the Arcadian to sink.

He has no known grave but is commemorated on Panel 11 Mikra Memorial, Mikra British Cemetery, Kalamaria, Greece. He is also commemorated on the Abbotshall Memorial Plaque.

HAYDON MELLOR

Private Haydon Mellor was born a son of Hirst and Mrs. Mellor of 127 Dunnikier Road, Kirkcaldy. He had a brother, Joseph and a sister. Haydon attended the High School and on leaving took up an apprenticeship as an organ builder with Peter Connocher & Co., Huddersfield.

However, he enlisted on his 18th birthday in the Gordon Highlanders, 8th/10th Battalion (although the School memorial shows the Black Watch) and was sent to France. Reports say that he had not been in the trenches an hour when he was struck by shrapnel and killed instantly. He was awarded the Victory Medal and the British War Medal.

Haydon was killed, aged 19 years, on 20th April 1918 and is buried in grave No. 1V.H.9 in Tilloy British Cemetery, Tilloy-Les-Mofflaines. He is also commemorated on a gravestone in Bennochy Cemetery.

WILLIAM H. CAMERON

Lance corporal William H. Cameron was the oldest son of William H. and Mrs. Cameron of 81 Dunnikier Road, Kirkcaldy. He attended the High School and on leaving he took up an apprenticeship with Mr. F. Stewart, Chemist, Commercial Street, Pathhead, Kirkcaldy.

He was still an apprentice when he enlisted in the Royal Army Medical Corps, 8th Field Ambulance, in November 1914. He was attached to Woolwich Arsenal Dispensary prior to being sent to France. He was awarded the Victory Medal and the British War Medal.

William died of wounds, aged 24 years, on 11th May 1917 in a hospital at St. Jean, Arras and is buried in grave No. V.D.33 in Faubourg d'Amiens Cemetery, Arras. He is also commemorated in Dunnikier Church Roll of Honour.

JAMES HEGGIE

L ance Corporal James Heggie was born in Abbotshall, Kirkcaldy, the son of Robert & Mrs. Heggie of 18 Balsusney Road, Kirkcaldy. He attended the High School but what career he followed on leaving is not known.

However, he enlisted in the Royal Engineers and was serving in 416th Field Company as a lance corporal at the time of his death. He was home on leave when he contracted influenza and he was taken to Craigleith Military Hospital for treatment. He was awarded the Victory Medal and the British War Medal.

James died of influenza on 2nd November 1918, aged 36 years, just nine days before the war ended.

He is buried in grave New (N) 206 in Abbotshall Parish Churchyard, Kirkcaldy. He is also commemorated on St. Andrews Church Memorial.

GEORGE FAIRHOLM MARSHALL

L ance corporal George Fairholm Marshall was born on 19th January 1896 in Kirkcaldy, the youngest son of James and Jessie Marshall of 8 Whytehouse Mansions, Kirkcaldy. James Marshall was a boot maker. George attended the High School where he was good at sports. On 10th November 1911 he was appointed an apprentice in the Pathhead branch of the National Bank of Scotland under a Mr. Inglis. He resigned in August 1914 but was re-instated as a clerk in the Kirkcaldy High Street Branch in January 1915.

He subsequently enlisted in the Royal Scots, 1st/9th Battalion and was promoted to lance corporal in the lewis gun section. He was sent to France and took part in the fighting on the Menin Road (Ypres) where he was wounded. He was awarded the Victory Medal and the British War Medal.

George died of his wounds on 23rd September 1917, aged 21 years, at 61 Casualty Clearing Station.

He is buried in grave No. V111.C.19 at Dozinghem Military Cemetery. His name is recorded on page 22 of the Royal Bank of Scotland Group Book of Remembrance.

DAVID MICHIE

Lance Corporal David Michie was born in 1892 the son of David and Mary Michie, of 'East Lynne', Whytehouse Avenue, Kirkcaldy. He attended the High School and on leaving entered his father's business of which he eventually took charge.

However, he enlisted in the Royal Scots, 2nd/10th Battalion, and served in France prior to being sent to North Russia. He was promoted to lance corporal. He sailed from Newcastle on 15th August 1918 and arrived at Archangel on 30th August. He was awarded the Victory Medal and the British War Medal.

The circumstances surrounding his death are confused. Army records state that he was killed in action, aged 26 years, on 7th October 1918 in Borok, Russia, but contemporary newspaper reports (Fife Free Press, 9th November 1918) say that he died on that date of heart disease. He has no known grave but is commemorated on the Archangel Memorial situated in Archangel Allied Cemetery, Russia. He is commemorated on a gravestone in Abbotshall Churchyard and on that church's memorial plaque.

DAVID TULLOCH

Lance Corporal David Tulloch was born in 1899 the only son of David and Jessie Tulloch, 36 High Street, Kinghorn. David Tulloch senior was a parish councillor and founder and president of Kinghorn Old Men's Hut. David attended the High School and on leaving he joined the Civil Service and was employed in Edinburgh.

He resigned and enlisted in the Gordon Highlanders,1st/6th Battalion. He was sent to France and was promoted to lance corporal. He was awarded the Victory Medal and the British War Medal.

David was killed in action on 23rd July 1918, aged 19 years. He is buried in grave No. B.30 at La Neuville-aux-Larris Military Cemetery. His name is commemorated on the family gravestone in Kinghorn cemetery and on Kinghorn War Memorial.

JAMES BALDIE

Private James Baldie was born at Largs, Ayrshire, the older son of John and Elizabeth Baldie, later of Royal Bank House, Markinch. He attended the High School but I have no details of his employment after leaving. He was a member of Balbirnie UF Church and was the first member of the congregation to be killed in action. His brother, John, also served and was killed in action on 6th November 1918, just five days before the armistice.

James enlisted in 1914 in the London Regiment (London Scottish) 14th Battalion (although the School magazine of December 1914 records that he enlisted in the 1st Battalion) and was soon to see action in France. He was awarded the Victory Medal, the British War Medal and the 1914/15 Star.

He was killed in action on 20th May 1915 aged 24 years and unusually, is buried in England in grave No.N.333 in Netley Military Cemetery, Southampton, Hampshire. His name is commemorated on Largs War Memorial and Markinch War Memorial. He is also commemorated on the London Scottish Regiment War Memorial.

ANDREW LESLIE BROWN

Private Andrew Leslie Brown was born the son of Andrew and Elizabeth Brown of 37 North Street, Leslie. He attended the High School but little else is known of his time there or of his life on leaving.

He enlisted in the Royal Army Medical Corps and was attached to the 41st General Hospital based in Greece. He was awarded the Victory Medal and the British War Medal.

Andrew died aged 30 on 16th February 1919, three months after the end of the war, and is buried in grave No. 1270 in Mikra British Cemetery, Kalamaria, Greece. The cause of death is not known. He is commemorated on Leslie War Memorial under the name 'Alexander Leslie Brown'.

PETER JOSEPH BYRNE

P rivate Peter Joseph Byrne was born the eldest son of Peter O. and Annie Byrne of Douglasfield, Abbotshall Road, Kirkcaldy. He attended the High School then Holy Cross Academy, Edinburgh, before studying for the priesthood at St. Francis Xaviers, Liverpool. By 1918 the family had moved to 13 Sang Road, Kirkcaldy.

He enlisted in the Royal Munster Fusiliers, 2nd Battalion (famous for its stand against the German army in the retreat from Mons in 1914 when it was all but wiped out) and was sent to France. He was awarded the Victory Medal and the British War Medal.

Peter was wounded, taken prisoner and died of his wounds the same day on 23rd March 1918 aged 20. He is buried in grave No. 11.D.6 in Honnechy British Cemetery and is commemorated in Edinburgh (Mount Vernon) Roman Catholic Cemetery.

ROBERT D. CURRIE

Private Robert Darney Currie was born the younger son of William and Mrs. Currie then of Leith where William was a merchant. The family moved later to 19 David the First Street, Kinghorn. Robert attended the High School and then George Watson's College, Edinburgh. He emigrated to Canada, aged 18years, in 1910 to take up employment with Canadian Pacific Railway. He was described as being a young man of great promise.

He enlisted in the Canadian Infantry (British Columbia Regiment) 29th Battalion and was eventually sent to France where he saw active service. He was awarded the Victory Medal and the British War Medal.

Robert was killed on 11th August 1916, aged 24, and is buried in grave No. 1.J.22 in Reninghelst New Military Cemetery. He is not commemorated on Kinghorn War Memorial, but his name is commemorated in George Watson's College Memorial, the Canadian Virtual War Memorial and on page 74 of the Canadian First World War Book of Remembrance.

CHARLES DUFF

Private Charles Ramsay Duff was the son of Mrs. Catherine Duff, formerly of 15 Normand Road, Dysart, and latterly of Balgarvie Cottage, Alexander Street, Dysart. He attended the High School and in 1910 he emigrated to Canada.

He enlisted in the Canadian Infantry (Alberta Regiment) 10th Battalion and on 19th March 1917 he was sent to France. He went "up the line" on the 27th April 1917 and was killed the following day having been at the front for a matter of hours. He was awarded the Victory Medal and the British War Medal.

Charles was killed on 28th April 1917 aged 36. He has no known grave but is commemorated on the Vimy Memorial. His name is also commemorated on Dysart War Memorial, the Canadian Virtual War Memorial and on page 231 of the Canadian First World War Book of Remembrance.

JAMES BURTON GIBSON

Private James Burton Gibson was born the son of Robert and Ann Burton Gibson of 39 Pratt Street, Kirkcaldy. He was educated at the West and Abbotshall primary schools before attending the High School. He was an all- round athlete and played rugby for the school's 1st XV. He was signed as an amateur by Raith Rovers Football Club and was part of the team which took part in the Scottish Cup final in the 1912/1913 season (Falkirk 2 – Raith Rovers 0). On leaving school he went to St. Andrews University where he graduated with an MA in 1913. In November that year he emigrated to New Zealand and took up a post as senior master at a school in Napier. He was a single man living at 11 Bellview Road, Mount Eden, Auckland.

On the outbreak of war he enlisted in the New Zealand Expeditionary Force (Auckland Regiment) and on 17th April 1915 was sent to the Dardanelles. He was awarded the Victory Medal, the British War Medal and the 1914/15 Star.

James died from wounds at sea on 5th September 1915, aged 26 and has no known grave. He is commemorated on the Lone Pine Memorial, Gallipoli, Turkey. He is also commemorated in the St Andrews University Roll of Honour, on the West End Congregational Church Plaque and on the Auckland War Memorial.

ROBERT GLASGOW

Trooper (private) Robert Glasgow was born on 11th May 1879 in Kirkcaldy the son of the Rev. Robert and Margaret Ker Glasgow of Invertiel Manse, Invertiel, Kirkcaldy. By 1915, however, the family had moved to 31 Abercorn Terrace, Portobello. Robert attended the High School and on leaving he became an apprentice engineer with Douglas and Grant Engineering, Dunnikier Foundry, Cupar. The company was founded by Robert Douglas (born 1822) and by the early 1900s had diversified into manufacturing rice milling machinery. On completion of his apprenticeship he went to India to work as an engineer in rice mills before travelling onwards to Sydney, Australia. He remained a single man.

His military career began as a volunteer in Kirkcaldy, continued in Rangoon where he served with the Royal Garrison Artillery and he finally enlisted on the 1st September 1914 in the Australian Infantry, 3rd Battalion, B Company. On 19th October 1914 he embarked on HMAT 'Euripides' from Sydney bound for Egypt where he saw service. He was eventually sent to Gallipoli. He was awarded the Victory Medal, the British War Medal and the 1914/15 Star.

Robert was killed in action on 27th April 1915 aged 36. He has no known grave and is commemorated on Panel 20 of the Lone Pine Memorial, Gallipoli. His name is also commemorated on a gravestone in Abbotshall Church yard , the Invertiel Parish Church Memorial and the Australian National War Memorial (Panel 36), Canberra, Australia.

FREDERICK COLIN GRAY

Private Frederick Colin Gray was born in 1892 in Logie, Fife, the eldest son of Donald and Elizabeth Gray. He had two sisters and a brother, Margaret, John and Elizabeth. His father was the minister of Pathhead United Free Church and the family lived at The Manse, St Ives, Loughborough Road, Kirkcaldy. He attended the High School and then Edinburgh University where he obtained an MA. When war broke out he was studying for the ministry.

He enlisted in the Argyll and Sutherland Highlanders, 1st/7th Battalion, and was eventually posted to France. Initial reports from France listed him as missing in action before his death was confirmed. He was awarded the Victory Medal and the British War Medal.

Frederick was killed in action on 15th November 1916 aged 24 years. He has no known grave and is commemorated on Pier and Face 15A and 16C of the Thiepval Memorial. His name is also commemorated on Pathhead Church Memorial Plaque and Windows, and in Edinburgh University Roll of Honour.

WILLIAM GRIERSON

Signaller William Grierson was born in 1897 the eldest son of Thomas and Christian Grierson of 4 Battery Place, Glasswork Street, Kirkcaldy. He attended the High School and some time after leaving he went to sea.

He enlisted in the Royal Naval Volunteer Reserve and qualified as a signaller. He was posted to HM Drifter "Our Allies", a net drifter of 91 tons launched in early 1915 and requisitioned by the Admiralty in August 1915. She was armed with a 57mm gun and was used as a net barrier tender in the Adriatic. He was awarded the Victory Medal and the British War Medal.

William died of influenza aged 21 years on the 22nd October 1918. He is buried in grave No. 3 at Gallipoli Communal Cemetery, Puglia, Italy. He is also commemorated on a gravestone in Abbotshall Churchyard and on Invertiel Parish Church Memorial Tablet.

ARCHIBALD BROWN LOW HARLEY

Trooper (private) Archibald Brown Low Harley was born the youngest son of Mr. & Mrs. HS Harley of 50 Townsend Place, Kirkcaldy. He attended the High School and on leaving was employed as an apprentice with the Commercial Bank of Scotland. In November 1912 he moved to the Pathhead Branch, still as an apprentice. He was described as being a fine musician who played the violin.

On the outbreak of war he enlisted as a trooper in the Fife and Forfar Yeomanry, B Squadron 1st/1st. His enlistment is recorded on page 13 of the December 1914 School magazine. In August 1915 the Squadron was dismounted and moved to Gallipoli via Egypt, landing on 26th September 1915. However, he seems to have remained in Egypt where he had caught typhoid fever and was confined to Zagazig Government Hospital, Port Said. His death is recorded on page 60 of the July 1916 School magazine. He was awarded the Victory Medal, the British War Medal and the 1914/15 Star.

Archibald died of typhoid fever aged 19 years on 18th November 1915. He is buried in grave No. 54 in Tel El Kebir War Memorial Cemetery, Egypt. His name is also commemorated on the Union Church Plaque, Kirkcaldy, in the Commercial Bank's Roll of Honour and on its War Memorial in Edinburgh.

CHARLES HARLEY

Private Charles Harley was born on 2nd August 1887 the son of Henry and Mary Harley of Ogilvie Street, Ferry Port on Craig, Fife. Henry was a seaman who worked on a dredger. Charles attended the High School and on leaving school he was employed in the office staff of Michael Nairn & Co., Linoleum Manufacturers, Kirkcaldy. However he left this employment to take over and run the newsagent business owned by his widowed mother at 1 Junction Road, Pathhead. He was married to Jeannie Gibb but had no children. He was a prominent golfer and held the Kirkcaldy and District Billiards Championship for several years. He was a good football player and played for Kirkcaldy Amateurs, Kirkcaldy United and Raith Rovers football clubs. He is described as being well known and highly esteemed in the town.

He enlisted in the Royal Scots, 13th Battalion, and was a member of the battalion shooting team. He played football for the battalion as well. In due course he was sent to France. He was awarded the Victory Medal and the British War Medal.

Charles was killed in action, aged 30, on 15th September 1916 and has no known grave. He is commemorated on Pier and Face 6D and 7D of the Thiepval Memorial. He is also commemorated on Bethelfield Church Memorial Plaque.

JOHN LANDELS IRELAND

Private John Landels Ireland was the older son of William L and Mrs Ireland of 23 Abbotshall Road, Kirkcaldy. He had a brother, Lockhart Landels Ireland *(qv)* and a sister. His father was an ironmonger with a shop in the High Street. He attended the High School but little is known of his life after that.

It is reported in the Fifeshire Advertiser of 5th August 1916, page 5, that he joined the Highland Cycle Brigade but due to lack of action he deserted and joined the Royal Irish Fusiliers (9th). It is recorded that he went to France where he was reported missing in action on the Somme (*ibid*).

John is believed to have been killed in action on the 1st July 1916. I have found no trace of his grave in Commonwealth War Graves Commission records or in Forces War Records. His name is commemorated on a gravestone in Bennochy cemetery, on Abbotshall Church Memorial Plaque and Whytescauseway Baptist Church Memorial Plaque.

LOCKHART LANDELS IRELAND

Private Lockhart Landels Ireland was the younger son of William L. and Mrs. Ireland of 23 Abbotshall Road, Kirkcaldy. He had a brother, John Landels Ireland *(qv)* and a sister. His father had an ironmonger's shop in the High Street. He attended the High School where he was found to have excellent literary skills and was something of an artist. On leaving school he took an interest in his father's business.

He enlisted in the Gordon Highlanders, 8th/10th Battalion and in due course was sent to France from where he sent regular reports to the local paper. He was seriously wounded in early 1916 and did not return to his unit until June, just before the Somme offensive. He lasted only a month before he was killed. He was awarded the Victory Medal and the British War Medal.

Lockhart was killed in action aged 29 years, on 25th July 1916 and is buried in grave No. V1.C.8 at Flat Iron Copse Cemetery, Mametz. He is also commemorated on a gravestone in Bennochy cemetery and on Whytescauseway Baptist Church Memorial Plaque.

ROBERT MURRAY KAY

Private Robert Murray Kay was born on 19th June 1893 at 7 Glebe Park, Kirkcaldy, the son of David Kennedy and Margaret Kay nee Burgess. His father was a draper at Port Brae, Kirkcaldy. His uncle was Robert Kay of West Kirklands, Hamilton, Lanarkshire and his aunt was Mrs. D. Kininmonth of Northall, Victoria Road, Kirkcaldy. He attended the High School and on leaving was employed by the Clydesdale Bank until 20th June 1914 when he joined the National Provincial Bank, South Shields branch as a clerk.

He enlisted in the Northumberland Fusiliers, 9th Battalion, and was eventually sent to France. His enlistment is reported on page 12 of the December 1914 School magazine. He was held in high esteem and had been recommended for a commission. His death was noted on page 60 of the July 1916 School magazine. He was awarded the Victory Medal, the British War Medal and the 1914/15 Star.

Robert was killed in action on 2nd October 1915. He has no known grave but his name is commemorated on Panel 8 and 12 of the Ypres (Menin Gate) Memorial. He is also commemorated on the Old Parish Church Memorial, the National Provincial Bank's Roll of Honour and on the Bank's war memorial in London.

JOHN LOUTTIT KILGOUR

Private John Louttit Kilgour was born on 13th September 1879 in Star, Kennoway, Fife, the son of John and Elizabeth L. Kilgour nee Bethune. His father was a master draper who lived at 217 Links Street, Kirkcaldy and his mother lived with her parents in Kennoway. His birth was registered twice, once in Kennoway and again in Kirkcaldy, which caused considerable confusion during research. However, John attended the High School and on leaving appears to have sought his fortune in Corstorphine, Edinburgh. He became a house painter and married his wife, Alice, born 1885 in Portobello. They had a son James born in 1910 and the family lived at 144 Victor Park Terrace, Corstorphine.

He enlisted in the Cameronians (Scottish Rifles) – although the school Memorial shows him to have joined the Black Watch – on the outbreak of war and he saw service in France and Flanders. He was awarded the Victory Medal, the British War Medal and the 1914/15 Star.

John was killed in action on 25th September 1915, just days after his 36th birthday. He has no known grave but is commemorated on Panel 57 to 59 of the Loos Memorial. His name is also commemorated on Corstorphine War Memorial.

RONALD KININMONTH

Private Ronald Kininmonth was born the younger son of William and Mary Kininmonth of Lothriebank, Wemyssfield, Kirkcaldy. His brother, William, survived the War having been awarded the Military Cross for conspicuous gallantry and died aged 43 in 1931. Ronald attended the High School and on leaving he joined R. Douglas & Co., aerated water manufacturers eventually becoming a partner in the firm.

He enlisted in the Royal Scots, 15th Battalion, in February 1916 and was in due course posted to France. He was awarded the Victory Medal and the British War Medal.

Ronald was killed in action aged 25 years, on 9th April 1917. He is buried in grave No. 1V.A.6 in Roclincourt Valley Cemetery. He is commemorated on the family gravestone in Bennochy cemetery and on St Brycedale Church Memorial Plaque.

SAMUEL THOMAS KINSMAN

Private Samuel Thomas Kinsman was born the son of Warwick and Margaret Kinsman of 3 Victoria Road, Kirkcaldy. He attended the High School and on leaving became a cashier and time-keeper for Messrs Douglas and Grant, steam engine and rice milling machinery manufacturers, at Rosyth.

Whilst still a teenager, he joined the Scots Guards, 1st Battalion, and was posted to France. He was awarded the Victory Medal and the British War Medal.

Samuel was killed in action, aged 19 years (one of the youngest of the School's casualties), on the 27th September 1918. He is buried in grave No. V111.F.18 at Flesquiercs Hill British Cemetery. He is also commemorated on a gravestone in Bennochy cemetery and on the Old Parish Church Memorial.

DAVID DAVIDSON LAING

Private David Davidson Laing, known as Davey, was born at Abbotshall the third son of David D. and Mary Laing of 16 James Grove, Kirkcaldy. His father was a draper in the High Street who died only 5 months after David. David attended the High School and on leaving was employed by the Commercial Bank. He was described as a modest and retiring young man. He was a keen golfer.

He enlisted in the Royal Scots, 9th Battalion, and was sent to France. He was wounded in action on 29th August 1916 with serious chest wounds and was transferred to the Western General Hospital, Cardiff. He was awarded the Victory Medal and the British War Medal.

David died of his wounds, with his mother by his side, on 15th October 1916, aged 21 years. He is buried in grave No. Raith 27 at Abbotshall Parish Churchyard.

ALEXANDER LEISHMAN

Private Alexander Leishman was the son of James and Mrs. Leishman of 97 Balsusney Road, Kirkcaldy. He attended the High School and on leaving joined the Civil Service as a clerk.

He enlisted in the Cameron Highlanders, 6th Battalion (formerly Lovat Scouts), in March 1917, whilst still a teenager (18 years old) and after training was sent to France. He was awarded the Victory Medal and the British War Medal.

Alexander was killed in action on 23rd July 1918, aged 19 years – another teenager who made the ultimate sacrifice. He has no known grave but is commemorated on Soissons Memorial.

ALFRED ATKINSON LENDRUM

Private Alfred Atkinson Lendrum was born on 9th September 1884 in Totnes, Devon, the only son of John H. and Alice M. Lendrum. His father was an Inland Revenue Excise officer who had been born in Ireland. Alfred had a younger sister, Gwendollyn, and the family lived initially at 11 Townsend Place, Kirkcaldy before moving to Denend, Kirkcaldy. Alfred attended the High School and on leaving aged 16 years he joined a local bank as a clerk. However, by 1911 he had left home to seek his fortune in America. He married Winifred Theresa Lendrum of 461 Sackett Street, Brooklyn, New York and they lived at 1523 73rd Street, Brooklyn. He was employed as a clerk.

On 28th August 1917 he enlisted in the Canadian Infantry (Central Ontario Regiment) 15th Battalion and volunteered for service overseas. He duly arrived in France and saw active service. He was awarded the Victory Medal and the British War Medal.

Alfred was killed in action on 2nd September 1918 a week before his 34th birthday. He is buried in grave No. 11.C.6 at Dominion Cemetery, Hendecourt-Les-Cagnicourt.

GEORGE CHARLES PENNYCOOK LENNOX

Private George Charles Pennycook Lennox was the son of John and Christine Lennox, 'Rosebank', 137 Dunnikier Road, Kirkcaldy. John Lennox was the general Manager of Pathhead and Sinclairtown Co-operative Society. George attended the High School and on leaving was employed as a land surveyor by Mr. Donaldson, the county Road Surveyor. He was described as a most estimable young man.

Whilst still a teenager, George enlisted in the Cameron Highlanders, 5th Battalion, and in due course was sent to Belgium. He was awarded the Victory Medal and the British War Medal.

George was 19 years old when he was killed on 20th April 1918. He is buried in grave No. V.C.24 at Haringhe (Bandaghem) Military Cemetery. He is also commemorated on Barony Church Memorial Plaque and on a gravestone in MacDuff Cemetery, East Wemyss.

CHARLES GOODE LANDELS LOVE

Private Charles Goode Landels Love was born the youngest son of George and Martha Landels Love of 4 Bennochy Terrace, Kirkcaldy. The family also had an address at White House, Dunshelt, Fife. He attended the High School and on leaving took up and served an apprenticeship with Messrs Phillip, Engineers. In 1907 he went to Canada where he continued to work as an engineer.

He enlisted in the Canadian Infantry, (Central Ontario Regiment) 4th Battalion, and volunteered for overseas service. In October 1916 he was wounded in the head from which he recovered. He was awarded the Victory Medal and the British War Medal.

George contracted trench nephritis (an acute disease of the kidneys caused by damp and conditions in the trenches) and was transferred to the Military Hospital, Endell Street, London, WC2 where he died aged 31 years on 2nd September 1917. He is buried in grave No. FF.89 at Bennochy Cemetery. He is also commemorated on Whytescauseway Baptist Church Memorial Plaque, the Canadian Virtual War Memorial and on page 277 of the Canadian First World War Roll of Honour in Ottawa.

JOHN SYDNEY MCKENZIE

Private John Sydney McKenzie was the only son of Donald and Grace McKenzie of 'Stewartville', 2 Berwick Place, Dysart. His father was a ship's captain and he had a number of sisters. He attended the High School and on leaving he took up a position as an apprentice with the Bank of Scotland, Dysart Branch, on 20th February 1912. Bank staff reports showed him to be turning into an excellent clerk and that he was very accurate with good hand writing.

He enlisted in the Black Watch (Royal Highlanders) 1st/6th Battalion, C Company and in due course was posted to Belgium. He was awarded the Victory Medal and the British War Medal.

John was killed in action on 2nd July 1917 aged 20 years. He is buried in grave No. 1.E.3 at Vlamertinghe New Military Cemetery, Ypres. His name is also commemorated on a gravestone in Dysart Cemetery and in the Bank of Scotland's Roll of Honour. He is commemorated on Dysart War Memorial under the name "John MacKenzie".

WILLIAM RICHARD MCPHERSON

Trooper William Richard Leitch McPherson was born on 15th January 1892, the only son of William George and Mary McPherson, 52 High Street, Kinghorn, Fife. His father conducted a grocery business from that address, although he was described as a labourer when he died. There was also one daughter from the marriage. William attended the High School and on leaving appears to have had several jobs. At one stage he was a railway porter with the North British Railway living at 96 High Street, Strathmiglo, but at the time of enlisting he was employed by the Patents Manufacturing Mills, Kinghorn.

He enlisted as a trooper in the Fife and Forfar Yeomanry but I have found no further information regarding his military service. His death certificate showed him to be a "pensioner" so it is possible that he was discharged due to ill health. It appears that he was entitled to be awarded the Victory Medal and the British War Medal.

William died aged 23 on 17th October 1916 at West Port, Falkland, of pthisis pulmonalis (a form of pulmonary tuberculosis causing progressive wasting of the body, cough and fever). He is buried in grave No. F.195 in Falkland Cemetery, the headstone being of standard Commonwealth War Graves Commission design. He is also commemorated on Kinghorn War Memorial.

JOHN M. MELVILLE

Private John M. Melville was born the youngest son of David and Mrs. Melville 19 Ava Street, Kirkcaldy. David was a coachbuilder. John attended the High School and on leaving was employed as a clerk by Messrs R. Heggie and Son, Linen Manufacturers. He was a keen sportsman and played football for Raith Rovers. Unfortunately requests for information from Raith Rovers FC produced no response.

He enlisted in the Black Watch (Royal Highlanders) 14th (Fife and Forfar Yeomanry) Battalion and was posted to Egypt. He was awarded the Victory Medal and the British War Medal.

John died of dysentery aged 23 on 12th November 1917. He is buried in grave No. F.338 in Cairo War Memorial Cemetery. His name is also commemorated on Longforgan War Memorial.

GEORGE MENZIES

Private George Menzies was born the eldest son of Thomas and Grace Menzies then of The Bungalow, 1 Beveridge Road, Kirkcaldy. He attended the High School but I have no further information about his career.

He enlisted in the Gordon Highlanders, 1st/7th Battalion and was posted to France where he saw active service. He was awarded the Victory Medal and the British War Medal. The circumstances of his death make interesting reading. His brother James learned that he had been wounded and set out to locate him. Enquiries of casualty clearing stations and hospitals proved negative so James decided to search the battlefield. This was done under heavy enemy fire but eventually James found George's body close to the enemy lines. He retrieved the body and brought it back to the British lines where he arranged for its burial which was conducted by Rev. JM Hunter, the minister of Abbotshall Church who was then serving as a forces chaplain. The full story is told in the Fife Free Press of 25th November 1916.

George was killed aged 31, on 13th November 1916. He is buried in grave No. 11.D.25 in Serre Road Cemetery No. 1. He is also commemorated on a gravestone in Bennochy Cemetery and on West End Congregational Church Memorial Plaque.

ROBERT DALE MILLIKEN

Private Robert Dale Milliken was born in 1895 in Kirkcaldy the younger son of Robert and Elizabeth Margaret Milliken, 20 Douglas Street, Kirkcaldy. Robert Senior was a photographer and there were two other children of the marriage, William Nillson Milliken who went on to be a photographer living at 3 Dalmeny Road, Edinburgh, and Ettie Nicholson Milliken. Robert attended the High School and on leaving became an apprentice engineer. He never married and appears to have lived at the family home prior to his death.

He enlisted in the Highland Cyclist Brigade. His enlistment is recorded on page 13 of the December 1914 School magazine, but I have found little else of his service record. In March 1917 he is recorded as being an army pensioner. He may have been entitled to the Victory Medal and the British War Medal.

Robert died aged 22, on March 20th 1917 in Edinburgh Royal Infirmary, of pernicious anaemia. I have been unable to find details of his grave or any of his details in the Scottish National War Memorial, but he is commemorated on the Old Parish Church Memorial Panel.

JOHN MONRO

Air mechanic 2nd Class John Monro was the eldest son of John and Isobel D. Monro of 108 Meldrum Road, Kirkcaldy. His father had his own business as a joiner / factor. John attended the High School where he was a member of the Officer Training Corps and was a piper in the school band and the Volunteer Training Corps pipe band. On leaving school he entered his father's business. He was a member of Kirkcaldy Swimming Club and Kirkcaldy Cricket Club. In his spare time he studied wireless telegraphy in Edinburgh.

He enlisted in the Royal Naval Air Service and was posted to HM Airship C7. He was awarded the Victory Medal and the British War Medal.

Still a teenager, John was killed in action aged 19 years on 21st April 1917 when his airship was shot down near North Foreland, Kent, by enemy aircraft. The airship was lost with all hands. He has no known grave but is commemorated on Panel 25, Chatham Naval Memorial, Chatham, Kent.

WILLIAM MORRISON

Private William Morrison was the son of James and Margaret Morrison, St. Kilda, Beveridge Road, Kirkcaldy. He attended the High School and the School magazine of December 1908, page 12, reports that he was appointed one of four corporals in the School's OTC. On leaving, he joined the Commercial Bank of Scotland as an apprentice in June 1909. In May 1914 he was moved to become accountant at Dunnikier Road Branch and in July 1914 he became accountant at Kirkcaldy West End Branch. He married Helen Burt Wilson formerly of 21 Archer Road, Penarth, Glamorgan. They set up home at 3 Nairn Street, Kirkcaldy. He was described as being well known and highly respected in the Burgh.

He enlisted in the Gordon Highlanders, 2nd Battalion and was eventually sent to France where he saw action on the Somme. He was awarded the Victory Medal and the British War Medal.

William was killed in action aged 23 on 1st July 1916. He has no known grave but is mentioned on Sp. Mem. C.12, the Gordon Cemetery, Mametz. He is also commemorated on a gravestone in Bennochy cemetery, in the Commercial Bank's Roll of Honour and on its war memorial in Edinburgh.

ROY SPEARS PIRIE

Signaller Roy Spears Pirie was born in 1895 the 2nd son of George and Mary Pirie, Townsend Villa, Townsend Crescent, Kirkcaldy. He attended the High School where he excelled at sports, winning the athletics championship, and representing the school at rugby. He played for the 1st XV. He was an officer in the school Cadet Corps. He spoke French and Spanish. On leaving school aged 18 years, he went to Canada where he roughed it for some time before going to New Zealand to take up farming. He settled in Rama Rama some 25 miles from Auckland. He is reported as being well known in Kirkcaldy.

However, in 1915 he decided to enlist and rode some 250 miles to join the New Zealand Expeditionary Force, Auckland Regiment, 2nd Battalion. In January 1916 he embarked on the vessel "Maunganui" at Wellington bound for Suez, Egypt. He then went to Belgium and finally France where he took part in the Somme offensive "on special work" . He was described as being a born soldier. He was awarded the Victory Medal and the British War Medal.

Roy was killed in action aged 21 years on 21st September 1916. He has no known grave but is commemorated on Caterpillar Valley (New Zealand) Memorial. He is also commemorated on St Brycedale Church Plaque and the Drury-Runciman Memorial, Auckland, New Zealand.

JAMES STRATTON ROBERTS

Private James Stratton Roberts was born the only son of Councillor James and Mrs. Isabella Roberts, Station Hotel, Sinclairtown, Kirkcaldy. He attended the High School and on leaving took up an apprenticeship with Thomas Dow and Sons, Solicitors, 120 High Street, Kirkcaldy. He was the third assistant of Thomas Dow to be killed in the war. He was secretary of Kirkcaldy United Football Club, Kirkcaldy's second senior club founded in 1901 and dissolved in 1916. They played at Scott's Park, now believed to be the site of a supermarket.

Whilst still a teenager James enlisted in the Black Watch (Royal Highlanders) 9th Battalion and was soon sent to Belgium. He was awarded the Victory Medal and the British War Medal.

James was struck by a shell and died instantly aged 19 years on 31st July 1917. He has no known grave but is commemorated on the Ypres (Menin Gate) Memorial Panel 37. He is also commemorated on a gravestone in Dysart Cemetery and on Pathhead Parish Church Memorial Plaques and Windows.

WILLIAM GEORGE ROBERTSON

Private William George Robertson was born on 21st May 1893 in Leslie, the only son of James and Catherine Robertson of Rosebank Terrace, Prinlaws, Leslie. They also had a daughter, Elizabeth. James was employed as a clerk. William attended the High School and on leaving joined the Union Bank, Leslie, but soon tired of this work and turned to farming on the Kinnieston Estate. He emigrated to Canada where he was engaged at an agricultural college in Nova Scotia.

He enlisted originally at Halifax, Nova Scotia on 19th November 1914 in to the Canadian Army Medical Corps but transferred to the Canadian Field Artillery, 2nd Brigade, 7th Battery. He was sent to France in 1915 where he saw active service. He was awarded the Victory Medal and the British War Medal.

William was killed in action aged 25 years, on 20th August 1918 the day before his brigade was withdrawn from the Front. He is buried in grave No. 1.B.52 in Bouchoir New British Cemetery. He is also commemorated on Leslie War Memorial, Gartly War Memorial Canada, the Canadian Virtual War Memorial and the Canadian First World War Book of Remembrance, page 492. His death was announced in Leslie Baptist Church.

JOHN MARSHALL RODGER

Gunner John Marshall Rodger was born in Kirkcaldy the second son of David and Margaret Rodger of Fife Arms, 250 St. Clair Street, Kirkcaldy. The other children were Agnes (a dress maker), David (a clerk), William (apprentice engineer) and Mary (school girl). David senior was a spirit merchant and the Fife Arms continues today as an "excellent local pub ...with a nice rustic beer garden". John attended the High School and on leaving became an apprentice grocer. He was a single man.

He enlisted in the Tank Corps, 3rd Battalion. Commonwealth War Graves Commission and Forces War records show his rank to be lance corporal, but the School War Memorial and the "Fife Free Press" of 16th November 1918, page 5, show his rank to be gunner. He was sent to France where he saw active service. He was awarded the Victory Medal and the British War Medal.

John died of wounds aged 25 years on 3rd October 1918. He is buried in grave No. 11.P.4 in Bellicourt British Cemetery. He is also commemorated on a gravestone in Barony Church yard.

PETER LEWIS ALE SHAND

Private Peter Lewis Ale Shand was born in Wemyss the youngest child and only son of James and Elizabeth Shand, Station House, West Wemyss. James Shand was a station master employed by the North British Railway. His other children were Anne, Susan, Elizabeth and Margaret. Peter attended the High School and on leaving served an apprenticeship with Messrs. J & JL Herd, Solicitors, 149 High Street, Kirkcaldy. He subsequently took up a position as an assistant factor / gamekeeper with the Lochiel Estate, Inverness. He was described as being a young man of great promise.

He enlisted in the Cameron Highlanders, 5th Battalion and was sent to the Front. He was awarded the Victory Medal and the British War Medal.

Peter was killed in action aged 24 years on 25th September 1915. He has no known grave but is commemorated on Panel 119 to 124 of the Loos Memorial. He is also commemorated on West Wemyss War Memorial.

WILLIAM ALASTAIR SANG

Private (sapper) William Alastair Sang was born on 28th October 1887 in Kirkcaldy, the younger son of William Drysdale Sang and Margaret Sang, of 12a Townsend Crescent, Kirkcaldy. William senior was a civil engineer. William attended the High School and on leaving followed his father's profession and became a civil engineer. Some time prior to 1911 he emigrated to Montreal, Quebec, Canada and took up employment with Canadian Railways. He remained a single man. His father predeceased him and his army record shows his next of kin as John Alfred Sang, 22, Stranmillis Gardens, Belfast. He was described as being a young man of much promise.

He enlisted in Montreal on 23rd March 1915 in the Canadian Railway Troops, Canadian Overseas Railway Construction Company and in due course was sent to France and Belgium. He was awarded the Victory Medal and the British War Medal.

William died aged 28 years on 25th March 1916. His Canadian Army records and the Canadian Expeditionary Force Burial Records show that he died at No. 10 Casualty Clearing Station from a self-inflicted gunshot wound to the head. The records do not say whether this was accidental or whether it was suicide. His gravestone gives no clue to the circumstances so the reader must make his/her own conclusions. He is buried in grave No. V.D.17 in Lijssenthoek Military Cemetery. He is also commemorated on a gravestone in Abbotshall Churchyard, the Canadian Virtual War Memorial and the Canadian First World War Book of Remembrance page 158.

ARCHIBALD SIMPSON

Private Archibald Simpson was the son of James and Mary Simpson of 18 David the First Street, Kinghorn. James was a seafaring man and at the time of his death was a ship's captain. Archibald attended the High School and on leaving he entered the Royal Bank of Scotland, Kirkcaldy Branch as an apprentice. He resigned in May 1913 and took up a position with the Anglo American Bank, London Branch, until August 1914. He was a member of Rosslands United Free Church, Kinghorn, and was a soloist in the church choir. He also sung in concerts for local charities. His father predeceased him and his mother moved to 10 Macduff Crescent, Kinghorn.

He enlisted in August 1914 in the County of London Regiment, 1st/20th Battalion and was posted to France and Belgium. He was awarded the Victory Medal, the British War Medal and the 1914/15 Star.

Archibald was killed in action on 25th September 1915 aged 23 years. He has no known grave but is commemorated on Panel 130 to 135 of Loos Memorial. His death is recorded on page 60 of the July 1916 School magazine. He is also commemorated on Kinghorn War Memorial.

JOHN SPEARS

Private John Spears was born on 30th March 1892 in Kirkcaldy, the only son of Thomas and Catherine Spears of 40 Lady Helen Street, Kirkcaldy. Thomas predeceased his son and his mother moved to Surrey Villa, 62 Trentham Road, Longton, Staffordshire. He was the nephew of a well known local cabinet maker, Matthew Spears. He attended the High School and on leaving in April 1909 took up an apprenticeship with the Commercial Bank of Scotland, Dunnikier Road Branch. In October 1911 he left to join a Canadian Bank in Vancouver.

In 1914 he enlisted in the Canadian Infantry, (Manitoba Regiment), 16th Battalion and volunteered for overseas service. He was awarded the Victory Medal, the British War Medal and the 1914/15 Star.

John died of wounds aged 24 years on 19th May 1915. He is buried in grave 111.D.50 in Bethune Town Cemetery. His death is recorded on page 60 of the July 1916 School magazine. He is also commemorated on Bethelfield Church Memorial Plaque, Longton War Memorial and Memorial Plaque, the Canadian Virtual War Memorial and the Canadian First World War Book of Remembrance, page 37, in Ottawa.

JAMES SPITTAL

Private James Nicol Spittal was born on 25th February 1895 in Markinch the youngest son of William and Elizabeth Spittal of 91 High Street, Markinch. William was a plumber by trade. James attended the High School and on leaving was employed in the clerical staff of Tullis Russell & Co., Papermakers, Markinch. His sister Isabella was likewise employed. They were employees during the opening of a small laboratory near the Auchmuty Gate and the building of a power station at the Markinch site (both 1912 – 1914).

He enlisted in the Black Watch (Royal Highlanders), 7th Battalion, in 1914 aged 19 years. His enlistment is reported on page 12 of the December 1914 School Magazine. He was sent to France and saw active service. He was awarded the Victory Medal, the British War Medal and the 1914/15 Star.

James was killed in action on 24th June 1915 aged 20 years. He has no known grave but is commemorated on Panels 24 to 26 on Le Touret Memorial. His death is recorded on page 60 of the July 1916 School magazine. He is also commemorated on Markinch War Memorial.

JOHN SMITH STENHOUSE

Private John Smith Stenhouse was born in Dundee the son of William and Susan Stenhouse of 411 High Street, Kirkcaldy. William was employed as a dock gate man. John attended the High School and on leaving held various jobs before emigrating to Australia in 1912. He became a miner in the copper mines around Brisbane. He was a single man whose religion was Methodist.

On 25th June 1915 he enlisted in the Australian Infantry, 25th Battalion, 5th Reinforcement at Brisbane and on 5th October 1915 he embarked on HMAT "Warilda" bound for Europe. He saw active service and served in the 9th Battalion and finally the 47th Battalion. He was awarded the Victory Medal and the British War Medal.

John was killed in action aged 30 years on 11th April 1917 during fighting at Bullecourt. He has no known grave but is commemorated on the Australian National Memorial Villers-Bretonneux, Panel No. 144. His name is also commemorated on a gravestone in Bennochy Cemetery.

BERNARD TOD

Private Bernard Douglas Tod was born in 1896 in Haddington, the only son of James and Elsie Tod later of St Brycedale Avenue, Kirkcaldy. James had been born in Edinburgh and was employed as a linoleum worker. Elsie had been born in Germany and their only other child, Elsie, had been born in London. The unusual spelling of the surname has been confirmed by birth certificate and census records. Bernard attended the High School and on leaving had travelled to London where he was employed by Messrs. Steel Bros. & Co. Ltd., engineers and oil prospectors. The family by this time had moved to 7 Bennochy Terrace, Kirkcaldy.

Whilst still a teenager, he enlisted in August 1914 in the London Regiment (London Scottish) 14th Battalion, 'A' Company and was posted to France where he saw active service. His enlistment is recorded on page 12 of the December 1914 School magazine. He was awarded the Victory Medal, the British War Medal and the 1914/15 Star.

Bernard was killed in action aged 19 years during the morning of 23rd December 1914, just two days before the unofficial "Christmas Truce". He has no known grave but is commemorated on Panel 45 Le Touret Memorial. His death is recorded on page 60 of the July 1916 School magazine under the surname "Todd". He is also commemorated on St Peters Church Memorial Plaque and the London Scottish War Memorial, Horseferry Road, London.

GEORGE E. TOOGOOD

Trooper George Erskine Twogood ("Toogood" on the School Memorial) was born on 14th June 1894 the youngest son of Charles William and Jane Ann Twogood of 175 Gorgie Road, Edinburgh. Charles was a self- employed laundry proprietor and there were three other children of the marriage, Robert, Arthur and Jane. By 1901 the family had moved to 13 Greenbank Terrace, Morningside, Edinburgh and Charles was a self-employed wholesale stationer. Some ten years later, by 1911, the family was living at "Dunsmure", Gallowgate, Kinghorn and the 1911 census records shows that the family name was recorded as "Toogood" (which caused problems for the researcher!). George attended the High School and on leaving he became a clerk at a local furniture factory.

He enlisted in the Household Cavalry, 1st Life Guards, and saw active service in France. He was awarded the Victory Medal and the British War Medal.

George died of wounds aged 23 years on 6th April 1917. He is buried in grave No. 1.H.2 at Duisans British Cemetery, Etrun. He is commemorated on Kinghorn War Memorial as "George E. Twogood".

PART THREE
APPENDICES

APPENDIX I

CWG CEMETERIES / MEMORIALS WHERE THE DECEASED ARE BURIED / COMMEMORATED

(Including numbers where appropriate)

Abbotshall Parish Churchyard (2)
Albert Communal Cemetery Extension
Archangel Memorial
Arras Memorial
Arras Road Cemetery
Barlin Communal Cemetery Extension
Bac-du-Sud British Cemetery
Bellicourt British Cemetery
Bethune Town Cemetery
Bouchoir New British Cemetery
Bouzincourt Communal Cemetery Extension
Brown's Copse Cemetery
Cabaret-Rouge British Cemetery
Cairo War Memorial Cemetery (2)
Cantara War Memorial Cemetery
Caterpillar Valley Cemetery
Caterpillar Valley (New Zealand) Memorial
Caudry British Cemetery
Charmes Military Cemetery
Chatham Naval Memorial
Cite Bonjean Military Cemetery
Combles Communal Cemetery Extension
Dominion Cemetery
Dozinghem Military Cemetery

Duisans British Cemetery

Dunkirk Town Cemetery

Falkland Cemetery

Faubourg D'Amiens Cemetery (2)

Flatiron Copse Cemetery (2)

Flesquieres Hill British Cemetery (2)

Gallipoli Communal Cemetery

Gordon Cemetery

Guards Cemetery Les Boefs

Guards Cemetery Windy Corner

Haringhe (Bandaghem) Military Cemetery

Honnechy British Cemetery

Houchine British Cemetery

Houplines Communal Cemetery Extension

Jerusalem War Cemetery

Kirkcaldy (Bennochy) Cemetery (2)

La Chaudiere Military Cemetery

La Clytte Military Cemetery

La Neuville-aux-Larris Military Cemetery

Le Touret Memorial (2)

Ligny-St. Flochel British Cemetery

Lijssenthoek Military Cemetery

Lone Pine Memorial (2)

Longuenesse (St. Omer) Souvenir Cemetery

Loos Memorial (3)

Maroeuil British Cemetery

Menen Communal Cemetery

Meteren Military Cemetery (2)

Mikra Memorial, Mikra British Cemetery (2)

Montecchio Precalcino Communal Cemetery Extension

Netley Military Cemetery

Niederzwehren Cemetery

Orchard Dump Cemetery

Oxford (Botley) Cemetery

Peronne Communal Cemetery Extension

Pont-d'Achelles Military Cemetery

Portsmouth Naval Memorial

Raperie British Cemetery

Reninghelst New Military Cemetery

Ridge Wood Military Cemetery

Roclincourt Valley Cemetery

Serre Road Cemetery No. 1

Serre Road Cemetery No.2

Sheerness (Isle of Sheppey) Cemetery

Soissons Memorial

Taranto Town Cemetery Extension

Tel El Kebir War Memorial Cemetery

Thiepval Memorial (8)

Tilloy British Cemetery

Trois Arbres Cemetery

Tyne Cot Memorial (2)

Valenciennes (St. Roch) Communal Cemetery (2)

Vermelles British Cemetery

Villers-Bretonneux Australian National Memorial

Vimy Memorial

Vlamertinghe New Military Cemetery

Windmill British Cemetery

Ypres (Menen Gate) Memorial (3)

Zuydcoote Military Cemetery

APPENDIX II

OTHER CEMETERIES / MEMORIALS COMMEMORATING THE FALLEN

(Including numbers where appropriate)

Abbotshall Parish Church Memorial   (5)

Abbotshall Parish Church Cemetery   (10)

Auchtertool Parish Church Memorial

Auckland War Memorial   (2)

Australian National War Memorial, Canberra

Bank of Scotland Roll of Honour

Barony Church Memorial Plaque   (3)

Barony Church Yard

Bethelfield Church Memorial Plaque   (4)

Canadian National Roll of Honour   (5)

Canadian Virtual War Memorial   (5)

Commercial Bank of Scotland Roll of Honour

Commercial Bank of Scotland War Memorial

Corstorphine War Memorial

Dunnikier Church Memorial   (3)

Dysart Cemetery   (6)

East Wemyss Macduff Cemetery

Edinburgh (Mount Vernon) Roman Catholic Cemetery

Galatown Church Roll of Honour

Gartly War Memorial, Canada

George Watson's College War Memorial   (8)

Holy Trinity Church Memorial, Rathmines

Invertiel Parish Church Memorial   (2)

Kinghorn Cemetery   (2)

Kinghorn Town War Memorial (6)

Kirkcaldy (Bennochy) Cemetery   (26)
Kirkcaldy Old Parish Church Memorial(6)
Kirkcaldy Town War Memorial
Largs War Memorial   (2)
Leslie War Memorial   (2)
London Scottish War Memorial
Longforgan War Memorial
Longton War Memorial
Markinch Town War Memorial(3)
Motherwell War Memorial
National Provincial Bank Roll of Honour
National Provincial Bank War Memorial
Pathhead Parish Church Memorial   (2)
Raith Church Memorial   (2)
Royal Bank of Canada Roll of Honour
Royal Bank of Canada War Memorial
Royal Bank of Scotland Group Book of Remembrance
Saskatchewan War Memorial
St Andrews Church Memorial   (3)
St. Andrews University Roll of Honour
St Andrews Western Cemetery
St. Brycedale Church Memorial Plaque (22)
St. Fillans War Memorial
St. Peters church Memorial   (3)
St. Serfs Church Memorial   (2)
Southampton Cenotaph
Union Church Memorial Plaque   (2)
West End Congregational Church Memorial   (4)
West Wemyss War Memorial
Whytescauseway Baptist Church Memorial Plaque   (3)

APPENDIX III

REGIMENTS JOINED BY THOSE NAMED ON THE WAR MEMORIAL

(Including numbers where appropriate)

Argyll and Sutherland Highlanders 7th Battalion
Argyll and Sutherland Highlanders 11th Battalion
Army Cycle Corps (Lowland)
Australian Infantry 3rd Battalion
Australian Infantry 25th Battalion
Black Watch (Royal Highlanders) 3rd Battalion
Black Watch (Royal Highlanders) 4th Battalion (3)
Black Watch (Royal Highlanders) 5th Battalion
Black Watch (Royal Highlanders) 6th Battalion
Black Watch (Royal Highlanders) 7th Battalion (8)
Cameron Highlanders (4)
Canadian Expeditionary Force (Alberta Regiment)
Canadian Expeditionary Force (British Columbia Regiment) (2)
Canadian Expeditionary Force (Field Artillery)
Canadian Expeditionary Force (Canadian Railway Troops)
Canadian Expeditionary Force (Central Ontario Regiment) (3)
Canadian Expeditionary Force (Manitoba Regiment) (2)
Canadian Expeditionary Force (Quebec Regiment)
County of London Regiment
Durham Light Infantry
Fife and Forfar Yeomanry (14th Black Watch) (5)
Gordon Highlanders 2nd Battalion (3)
Gordon Highlanders 4th Battalion (2)
Gordon Highlanders 6th Battalion
Gordon Highlanders 7th Battalion

Gordon Highlanders 9th Battalion

Gordon Highlanders 10th Battalion (2)

Highland Cycle Brigade (2)

Highland Light Infantry (2)

Kings Royal Rifle Corps

Lifeguards

London Regiment (London Scottish) (3)

Machine Gun Corps (2)

Manchester Regiment

New Zealand Expeditionary Force (Auckland Regiment) (2)

Northumberland Fusiliers

Royal Air Force (3)

Royal Army Medical Corps (4)

Royal Dublin Fusiliers

Royal Engineers (4)

Royal Field Artillery

Royal Flying Corps (4)

Royal Irish Fusiliers

Royal Munster Fusiliers

Royal Naval Air Service (2)

Royal Naval Volunteer Reserve (3)

Royal Scots 2nd Battalion (2)

Royal Scots 9th Battalion (2)

Royal Scots 11th Battalion

Royal Scots 13th Battalion (2)

Royal Scots 14th Battalion (2)

Royal Scots 15th Battalion (6)

Royal Scots Fusiliers 4th Battalion

Royal Scots Fusiliers 9th Battalion

Scots Guards 1st Battalion

Seaforth Highlanders

Tank Corps

APPENDIX IV

KIRKCALDY STREET INDEX SHOWING NUMBER OF HIGH SCHOOL DEATHS

STREET NAME	NUMBER OF DEATHS
Abbotshall Road	4
Ava Street	2
Balfour Street	1
Balsusney Road	3
Balwearie Road	1
Bennochy Terrace	2
Berwick Place	1
Beveridge Road	1
Blinkbonny	1
Carlyle Road	3
Denend	1
Douglas Street	1
Dunnikier Road	7
Forth Avenue North	1
Forth Park	1
Forth Street	2
Giffen Park	1
Glasswork Street	1
High Street	5
Invertiel	1
James Grove	1
Junction Road	1
Lady Helen Street	1
Lady Nairn Avenue	1

STREET NAME	NUMBER OF DEATHS
Loughborough Road	3
Meldrum Road	1
Milton Road	4
Nicol Street	2
Normand Road	1
Pratt Street	1
Roseberry Terrace	1
Sang Place	1
Sang Road	1
Seaview	1
St Clair Street	1
Swan Road	3
Townsend Crescent	2
Townsend Place	4
Victoria Road	4
Wemyss Field	1
Wemyss Park	1
West Albert Road	5
Whytehouse Avenue	1
Whytehouse Mansions	1
Windmill Road	1

The list does not include those pupils who lived outside Kirkcaldy such as Leslie, Markinch, Kinghorn, Burntisland, Falkland or overseas.

Whilst any death must have been hard to bear, West Albert Road must have suffered worst. It is a very short road, some 150 yards long, yet had to suffer the deaths of five of its brightest residents. Milton Road with four deaths and Swan Road with three must have felt similar pangs but Dunnikier Road, on the other hand, along with the High Street, Abbotshall Road, Loughborough Road and Balsusney Road were long roads where the deaths were less likely to affect the whole street. The area bounded by Milton Road, Abbotshall Road, Victoria Road, Dunnikier Road and the High Street (less than a mile long and a third of a mile wide)bore most of the deaths.

MAP OF KIRKCALDY CIRCA 1914

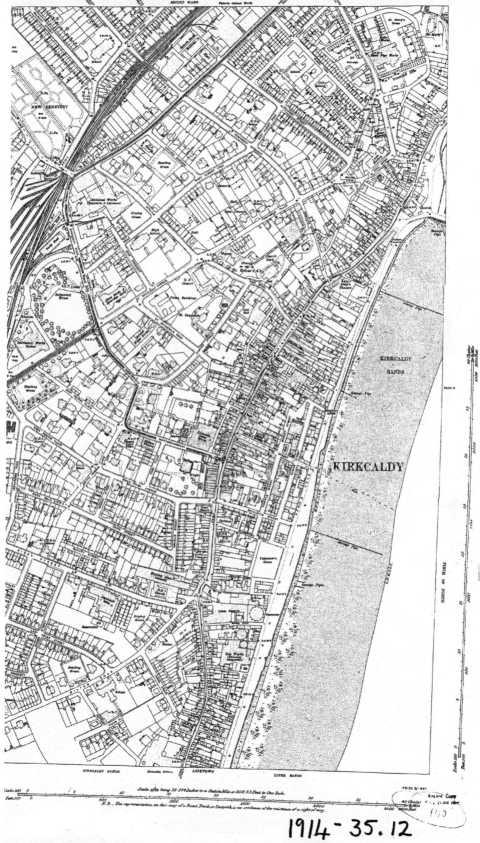

KIRKCALDY

KIRKCALDY
SANDS

FIRTH OF FORTH

NEW CEMETERY

SECOND WARD

1914 - 35.12

APPENDIX VI
PHOTOGRAPHS OF LOCAL WAR MEMORIALS

Kirkcaldy Town Memorial

Dysart War Memorial

Kinghorn War Memorial

Leslie War Memorial

Markinch War Memorial

Nine small crosses placed at the foot of the Leslie War Memorial

Kirkcaldy High School War Memorial

Kirkcaldy Town War Memorial Detail of Central Panel

APPENDIX VII

THE CAMPAIGN MEDALS OF WORLD WAR I

The British War Medal

In 1919 The British War Medal (1914-1920) was authorised for award to service personnel and civilians who had served between 5 August 1914 and 11 November 1918 and who had either entered a theatre of war, or rendered approved service overseas. It was extended to include Service in Russia during the 'North Russia Intervention' of 1919 and 1920.

In total 6,390,000 silver medals were awarded and 110,000 bronze medals, the latter principally to the Malay, Chinese and Indian labour battalions.

The Victory Medal

Also known as the Inter-Allied Victory medal, the Victory Medal and the British War Medal together were nicknamed Mutt and Jeff. The Victory Medal 1914-1919, was authorised in 1919 for issue to those eligible personnel who were mobilised in any service and entered a theatre of war between 5 August 1914 and 11 November 1919.

Over 6,334,000 medals were awarded. It was never issued in isolation, but to those who were in receipt of the 1914 Star, the 1914-15 Star and to most of those who received the British War Medal.

The 1914 Star and the 1914/15 Star

Eligibility was for either the 1914 Star or the 1914/15 star, (not both) which when issued with The British War Medal and the Victory medal were known affectionately as Pip, Squeak and Wilfred, after a popular Daily Mail comic strip. The 1914 Star was authorised in 1917 for issue to the officers and men of the British Forces who served ashore in France and Flanders between 5th August and 22nd November 1914, mostly those of the British Expeditionary Force known as 'the old Contemptibles'. An additional clasp was awarded to those who had been within range of enemy fire during the period and this became known as the Mons Star. The 1914/15 Star, was issued to those who served in another operational theatre between 5th August and 22nd November 2014 or during the extended period from the 23rd November 1914 to December 2015.

BIBLIOGRAPHY

Books, Booklets, Newspapers

Doyle, Peter and Foster, Chris – *British Army Cap Badges of the First World War.* Shire Publications, Oxford , 2012

Klak E. and Klak J. – *The Register of the Fife Fallen in the Great War 1914-1919 Volume 1 Kirkcaldy and Dysart Fallen* Fife Military History Society, Thornton 2002

Wood, Lewis N. – *These Men of Banstead.* Banstead History Research Group

Wylie, Michael – *The War Poets An Anthology.* Pitkin Publishing, Andover, 1992

Fife Free Press 1914-1919

Fifeshire Advertiser 1914 – 1918

Friends of Kirkcaldy High School Magazine 2000, FoKHS 2000

Kirkcaldy High School (Elementary Department) Log Book 1906–1922

Kirkcaldy High School Magazines – June 1908, December 1908, December 1914, December 1915, July 1916, December 1916.

Websites (Selected)

Commonwealth War Graves Commission – www.cwgc.org

Forces War Records – www.forces-war-records.co.uk

Library and Archives Canada – www.collectionscanada.gc.ca

National Archives, Kew – www.nationalarchives.gov.uk

The National Archives of Scotland – www.nas.gov.uk

Scotlands People – www.scotlandspeople.gov.uk

The Scottish War Memorials Project – www. scottishmilitaryresearch.co.uk

Western Front Association – www.westernfrontassociation.com